CASSANDRA EASON

COMPLETE GUIDE
to

TAROT

CASSANDRA EASON

COMPLETE GUIDE

to

TAROT

THE CROSSING PRESS
FREEDOM, CALIFORNIA

Copyright © 1999 Cassandra Eason
Interior design by Zena Flax
Printed in the USA

First published in the UK by Judy Piatkus (Publishers)
Limited, 1999

For information on bulk purchases or group discounts for this
and other Crossing Press titles, please contact our Sales Manager
at 800/777-1048.

Visit our website on the Internet: **www.crossingpress.com**

Library of Congress Cataloging-in-Publication Data
Eason, Cassandra.
    Complete guide to the tarot / by Cassandra Eason.
        p. cm.
    Includes bibliographical references and index.
    ISBN 1-58091-068-8 (pbk.)
    1. Tarot. I. Title.

BF1879.T2 E27   2000
133.3'2424--dc21   99-058264

Contents

Introduction   **1**

Part 1 – Tarot Essentials

1 The Major Arcana – A Journey of Self-discovery   **21**

2 The Court Cards – The Key to Relationships   **47**

3 The Minor Arcana – A Map Through Life   **74**

4 Choosing a Spread   **100**

Part 2 – Taking the Tarot Further

5 Fortune Telling and the Tarot   **119**

6 The Tarot and the Zodiac   **127**

7 Crystals and the Tarot   **146**

8 The Tarot and Psychic Development   **163**

9 The Kabbalah and the Tarot   **177**

10 The Tarot and Numerology   **206**

11 The Tarot and Magic   **223**

Appendix 1: Turning Professional   **241**

Appendix 2: Tarot Packs   **245**

Further Reading   **247**

Index   **248**

Introduction

The Tarot – From Microcosm to Macrocosm and Back Again

Take a pack of Tarot cards in your hand and you hold a treasury of magical powers. Even if you never learned the set meanings of individual cards nor carried out a single reading, you would still discover in each image, like the pages of a richly illustrated book, symbols that kindled deep emotion and insight, connecting with your life both on the everyday plane and with the realms of the soul. For Tarot cards are a tool, not only of divination, but also for exploring the psyche and other dimensions, past, present and future, by a natural route that begins in the imagination and ends who knows where.

This book offers to those unfamiliar with the Tarot both specific card meanings, and both basic and more complex card layouts. Almost from the start you can give readings for yourself and others, discovering through the cards the important influences on your actions and potential paths to happiness; for the more experienced reader, each section offers suggestions to undertake a personal journey of spiritual evolution and explore relationships using the Tarot images.

For the cards offer access to an interrelated system of psychic experiences, following avenues suggested by earlier occultists. For example, the Tarot can be linked to the **Kabbalah** (the ancient Hebrew mystical system), astrology, crystals and basic numerology. The cards can also be

A medieval engraving representing Venus

used as a focus for meditation, leading to astral projection and past life regression.

And, in themselves, the cards offer a complete system for magic and ritual and a means of developing hidden strengths and qualities.

This is mainly a practical book for personal exploration and enlightenment and one that can be used as a template for future development. I have been studying the Tarot for over ten years – using and demonstrating the cards regularly on radio, television and in private readings. I have written several books on the Tarot as well as other major forms of divination, magic and ritual, exploring the historical, spiritual and psychological contexts in depth. Yet each time I feel I am approaching complete understanding, I turn another corner or enter a new phase of my life and an unexplored vista waits. For this reason, I have suggested a variety of other Tarot and ritual books and a wide selection of packs so that you too can follow the path in your own way and your own time.

The Tarot is a living craft which evolves with those who use it and you will create your own unique approach in which the cards become not repositories of truth in themselves, but rather a series of pathways to the treasury of universal wisdom within. In knowledge you will then move away from books and the methods of others and follow your heart – the true teacher.

The Origins of the Tarot

The history of the Tarot is shrouded in myth and mystery. Throughout the centuries these cards, through their archetypal images that span space and time, have offered answers to people's deepest needs and questions. So in a sense all the explanations for the origins of the Tarot have elements of truth. The cards contain the same wisdom expressed by the Ancient Egyptians, the Chinese and Indian cultures, the magical insights carried by the Romanies on their long wanderings across Asia into Europe, the hidden formulae of the alchemists and the secret esoteric teachings of persecuted medieval religious sects.

For the concepts behind any valid divinatory system are central to the human condition and in this most exciting, mysterious and spiritual form they find expression in universal images: mother, father, the divine child, the wise man, the virgin, the hermit, the hero, the lover and the trickster, the quest for immortality and enlightenment, as well as more traditional virtues of endurance, patience, moderation and justice.

Tarot cards in their present form seem to be a medieval creation, although the images and themes are much older. The Bibliothèque Nationale in Paris has seventeen ornate cards, sixteen of them Tarot Trumps, originally believed to have been made for Charles VI of France around 1392, but now thought to be Italian and dating from about 1470.

One suggestion is that Tarot cards sprang from the north of Italy, in the valley of the Taro River which is a tributary of the River Po. This could have influenced the Italian name for the cards Tarrochi and the French name Tarot.

The modern Tarot pack comes directly from an Italian version, the Venetian or Piedmontese Tarot which has twenty-two trumps. The same form is found in the still popular French pack called the Tarot of Marseilles. Both designs were in general use by about 1500 in Northern Italy and France. The four suits represented different strata of society: the Swords were the aristocracy; Cups or Chalices the clergy and monastic orders; Pentacles or Coins the merchants; and Wands or Batons the peasants.

The Egyptian God, Thoth

In 1781, a time when Egypt was seen as the source of all knowledge, Antoine Court de Gebelin, a French Protestant clergyman who became fascinated by the occult, found some friends playing with Tarot cards. He identified the cards as containing the secrets of the priests of Ancient Egypt, the lost Egyptian magical wisdom written by Thoth, the Egyptian god of inspired written knowledge, encoded in Tarot symbolism to protect this knowledge from invading barbarians. The Arabic word

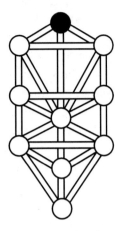

The Kabbalah Tree of Life

Tariqua (the way of wisdom) bears some resemblance to Tarot and the Ancient Egyptian word *Ta-rosh* means the Royal Way. Some believe that the Tarot was named after Taueret, the Egyptian hippopotamus goddess who was the protective deity of childbirth, known to the Greeks as Thoeris, The Great One. Taueret was said to have given birth to the Tarot. A third root was seen in the Kabbalah, the source of Hebrew esoteric wisdom; Torah is the Hebrew name for the first books of the Old Testament.

The Order of the Golden Dawn, a mystical order to which the poet W. B. Yeats belonged, attached a great deal of significance to the Latin word *ROTA*, meaning Wheel, engraved on the Wheel of Fortune card. Rota is an anagram of both Tora(h), and Taro. By learning the Tarot, one can step off the Wheel of unremitting Fate.

In 1856 Eliphas Levi made the first connections between the Tarot and the Kabbalah. He linked the twenty-two Major Arcana cards with the twenty-two letters of the Hebrew alphabet that each possessed inherent esoteric significance as pathways on the Tree of Life. These letters connected each card with specific ways to enlightenment. Eliphas Levi was the pseudonym for Alphonse Louis Constant. Born in 1810, he was first a Catholic priest, then a teacher and writer and became interested in the study of magic and coined the word occult (meaning 'what is hidden').

Other theories link the origin of the name Tarot with the Celtic Tara, the sacred Hill of the High Kings of Ireland from ancient times until the sixth century AD. This view was given credence by Robert Graves, the historian and novelist, who believed that the twenty-two Tarot trumps were derived from the Tree Alphabet of the Celts with its twenty-two symbols.

The greatest influence on modern Tarot reading is Arthur Edward Waite who in 1891 joined the Order of the Golden Dawn. He commissioned the artist Pamela Coleman-Smith to draw the pack for him and the result was the Waite Tarot pack with its richly illustrated Minor

Arcana intended to promote visions as well as being used for divination. Waite associated the four suits with the four sacred objects of the Holy Grail quest and many of his cards reflect the romantic Arthurian background of the Grail legends. The Waite pack, the first to contain images depicting the meanings of the Minor cards, became the template for countless later decks.

But it was not until the 1960s, with the rise of the interest in New Age phenomena on both sides of the Atlantic, that the Tarot reached a wider audience and now many people from all walks of life regularly read Tarot cards for themselves, family and friends. An increasing number of professional readers work in locations from city to village, their premises varying from a back room in an ordinary house or apartment to a quasi-medical consulting room. However, although there are Tarot phone lines in almost every newspaper and journal, even now many television and radio networks in the UK do not allow Tarot card readings on air, although they routinely accept astrology, runes, clairvoyance and mediumship. There is also some undeserved hostility towards the Tarot cards that stems mainly from the fear of the Death, Devil and Tower of Destruction cards as literal harbingers of evil and destruction, even when these cards are treated purely psychologically and their innate overriding positive aspects emphasised.

But the Tarot continues to flourish and there are now hundreds of designs to choose from (see Chapter 4 on Choosing a Spread) ranging from fine art to cartoons. But almost all have retained the vision of those early designers and the underlying symbolism continues to grant access to our own and the universal well of wisdom, as it did for our forebears.

Accessing the Power of the Tarot

Some people believe an external force controls their apparently random choice of cards in a divinatory reading, whether it be their own spirit or angelic guide, or that of the person who is reading for them. I believe we are using internal powers of intuition and inspiration. The psychologist Gustav Carl Jung stated that our collective unconscious gave us access to the experiences and accumulated wisdom of humanity, and took us beyond the confines of linear time and space. This level of experience enables us to move beyond the present and past to glimpse not a fixed future, but possibilities and choices just over the horizon. He also believed in meaningful coincidences and coined the term 'synchronicity'. According to his theories, the Tarot cards we select are prompted by some inner stirring that will become manifest in the external world.

Another theory says that we carry within us a Tribal Voice or Great Memory, similar to Jung's collective unconscious. It may be that on the genetic level we carry the memories and experience of our ancestors as they absorbed the knowledge of those who went before them and so we have access to a vast repository of learning from the different cultures from which we ultimately claim descent.

Some kind of telepathic power may influence our apparently random selection of cards, perhaps akin to telekinesis where the mind can influence inanimate objects, so that the cards chosen are relevant to issues we had not even consciously realised were troubling us. Even for those sceptics who argue that the selection is entirely due to chance, the Tarot is still valid because even using a small number of cards, for example only the Major Arcana in a spread of five cards, you would still have a large combination of images, all of which address vital issues in the life of any individual.

I am convinced by the seemingly uncanny accuracy of countless readings I have witnessed that the Tarot is far more than a psychic form of the psychological ink-blot test whereby you interpret abstract shapes to get in touch with your problems, because time and time again a combination of cards are dealt that do encapsulate all the aspects of an issue — and in their interpretation offer a previously unconsidered solution.

Tarot Rituals – Empowering and Cleansing Your Pack

When you first buy your Tarot pack, simple rituals can offer both psychic protection and energise your cards, based on the ancient elements of Earth, Air, Fire and Water that were once regarded as the composition of all life (see Chapter 11 the Tarot and Magic). Place your cards in a circle on a strong, fireproof, circular metal tray so that the seventy-eight pictures are uppermost and each one is touching. Begin in the north. Create first a circle of sea salt sprinkled clockwise around the outside of the card circle, and say:

The Lotus Flower was the Egyptian Symbol for the earth

> *Mother Earth, keep my feet on the ground while my inspiration soars, so that I never lose connection with your strong roots. Give shelter to all my divination.*

Light an incense stick of pine or rosemary for energy and clarity of thought, or sandalwood for psychic and healing powers, and with it draw a clockwise circle of smoke along the line of your salt circle, saying:

> *Father Sky, endow me with keen perceptions and searching insights that I may see and speak true and not be lulled by illusion.*

Next light a golden, yellow or red candle and carefully drip a trail of wax on the circle of salt, clockwise, saying:

> *Creative and inspiring Brother Fire, give me the power to make connections between the seen and unseen that I may see possibilities where none are apparent and find hope even in the midst of negativity.*

Finally, using a dish of water steeped with rose petals or rose or lavender essential oil, sprinkle a circle of water clockwise enclosing the salt and wax circle. This will create a triple sacred circle. Say:

Gentle Sister Water, endow me with sensitivity, compassion and intuitive understanding that my words may be uplifting and healing, alleviating sadness and comforting loneliness.

Leave the tray with the cards on a window ledge for a sun and moon cycle of twenty-four hours. Let the candle and incense burn away in a safe place and bury the salt and wax in the earth or dispose of it.

You may want to keep your Tarot cards wrapped in dark silk in a drawer when you are not using them.

Psychic Protection

Avoid carrying out divinatory or indeed any psychic work when you are feeling exhausted or negative. Your explorations should be entirely harmonious and positive. However, because you do become very sensitive to atmospheres the more you evolve psychically, it is important to establish a psychic space in which to work and to close down this area after you have finished so that you are not kept awake all night.

Even in a public place, you can draw a circle of protection around yourself in your mind's eye by visualising a glowing amber crystal or brilliant crystal quartz radiating clockwise from the north that encloses you in golden light. When you have finished giving a reading, close down the circle in an anti-clockwise direction by picturing a dark crystal such as a smoky quartz or obsidian overwriting the golden light and leaving you at peace. If you are alone, you can use actual crystals to draw and uncast the circle.

If you are reading for someone else, you can enclose them in a visualised separate circle of protection, so that if they do have negative vibes through sadness or anxiety, these are contained and dispelled at the end of the reading, without entering your personal sphere.

When you have read your cards for someone else, pass a crystal pendulum or an amethyst over your cards to draw out any negative feelings and then wash the pendulum or crystal under running water. Afterwards rest the pendulum or crystal in black silk for a while.

INVOKING PSYCHIC PROTECTION IN A MORE FORMAL WAY

Some people invoke four archangels to stand in each corner of the room before beginning a Tarot reading or any psychic work using Tarot cards. Create your own images of these beings of light.

- **Raphael** is the travellers' guide and the angel who offers healing to the planet and to humankind and all creatures on the face of the earth, in the skies and waters. He is also guardian of the young. He is usually depicted with a pilgrim's stick, a wallet and a fish, showing the way and offering sustenance to all who ask. Raphael stands in the north. You can use a green candle, jade or aquamarine to invoke his protection.
- **Uriel**, whose name means Fire of God, is associated with earthquakes, storms and volcanoes and is the Archangel of Salvation. Believed to have given alchemy to humankind, he also imparted the wisdom of the Kabbalah to Hebrew mystics. He stands in the east. You can use a yellow candle, carnelian or amber to invoke his protection.
- **Michael**, the warrior and Archangel of the Sun, appeared to Moses as the fire in the burning bush and saved Daniel from the lion's den. As commander of the heavenly hosts, he is usually pictured with a sword. Michael's position is in the south with the noonday sun. You can use a gold candle, a citrine or pure crystal quartz to represent his protection.
- **Gabriel**, the Archangel of the Moon, the messenger

archangel and the heavenly awakener, appears many times in the Bible, visiting the Virgin Mary and her cousin Elizabeth, mother of John the Baptist, to tell them that they were to bear sons who would lead humankind to salvation. He is usually pictured holding a sceptre or lily. Gabriel stands in the west. You can use a silver candle, a moonstone or fire opal to represent his protection.

Remember afterwards to thank your psychic guardians and to visualise them moving further away to watch you through the night. If you lit candles, blow them out in the reverse order of lighting, sending the protective light to any people you have read for who are distressed or lonely.

Wash any crystals you used in running water and leave them to grow strong in moon and sunlight. Alternatively ask your personal guides, God, the Mother Goddess or a named chosen deity for protection, or invoke the protection of the benign powers of the universe before beginning psychic work. You can light four pure white pillar candles beginning in the northernmost corner to invoke the protection of light, again extinguishing them after use.

A representation of the Earth Mother

Reading for Others

A Tarot reading is one of the most intimate psychological and spiritual experiences you can undertake, so the rapport between you and the person for whom you are reading is the key to a meaningful and positive experience. Here are some suggestions you may find helpful.

- If the questioner is not familiar with the cards, allow him or her to hold the pack and turn over the cards. You can briefly explain meanings. This is a good way of letting the questioner imprint his or her consciousness on the cards.
- Take the pack yourself and shuffle it, so absorbing the psychic impressions of the questioner, asking the person for whom you are reading to think of a question or issue and concentrate on it.

- Give the cards back to the questioner to shuffle and ask him or her, still concentrating on the question, to select the required number of cards one at a time from anywhere in the pack.
- You can then assign the cards to the appropriate positions. If the cards do not have particular position meanings, you can ask the questioner to turn over the cards in the order that feels right, but otherwise it is easier to turn the cards yourself.
- Ask the questioner if he or she will tell you about the issue. It is hard to get away from the concept that a reader should know the problem telepathically, but that can actually detract from a true dialogue and create false expectations that the reader can also determine the best course of action for the questioner.
- Once you have explained the basic card meanings, ask the questioner what the cards seem to be saying in relation to his or her life. It is surprising how quickly even a newcomer to the cards will, in a sympathetic environment, apply the images to his or her own situation with virtually no help and then you will know you have succeeded.

Whether you are a professional reader or a friend, it can be hazardous to give advice either psychically or psychologically unless you are prepared to help the other person follow through any changes you suggest and that can mean support for months or even years. It is tempting if someone is sad or lonely to promise riches or new love, but it may be better to steer the person towards making small changes.

Reading for Yourself

It is certainly not unlucky to read for yourself and the cards offer a way of holding on to those fleeting insights and inspirations that emerge in states of altered consciousness. Tarot readings have been described as laying out your dreams and for me the Tarot is primarily a personal guide.

THE FOOL.

A Major Arcana card

Many busy people, especially women, make room in their lives for an evening Tarot time once or twice a week, or when there is an important decision to be made. This they describe as a sacred place in which they can reaffirm their own identity. If possible set aside for yourself a special table or place with candles and your crystals around. Light a divinatory incense such as frankincense or sandalwood or use an oil burner and wear something loose and warm.

When you have finished your reading, sit by candlelight reflecting on the cards, play some gentle music, and let the images come and go.

CHOOSING YOUR CARDS OF THE DAY

As well as this special time, you can incorporate the Tarot into your everyday world, each morning. Find the time by waking earlier or relinquishing a chore others could do.

Divide the whole pack into two piles, one for the Major Arcana and the other the Minor (these are explained briefly later in this chapter, and fully in the next three chapters of the book). You can do this the night before if you are very short of time in the morning.

In the morning shuffle each Arcana and from the Major select one card without looking at it. This will give you the underlying influence or theme of the day.

Take a second card from the Minor pile, again without looking. This card refers to the major event of the day and can contain an inbuilt strategy. If it is a Court card it refers to a person or an aspect of yourself which will be prominent.

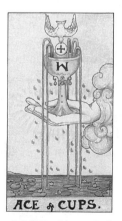

ACE of CUPS.

A Minor Arcana card

Note down your cards of the day and you may find that certain ones appear frequently, indicating an area where attention will be repaid with rich rewards or an obstacle that you need to overcome.

Reversed Cards and Significators

Some Tarot readers consider a card dealt upside down has a weakened or opposing meaning. However, in my experience this is just because the card was returned the incorrect way to the pack during an earlier reading. All the cards contain positive and negative significance within them according to the context of the whole reading.

Traditional readers also sometimes assign a significator or significant card, usually a Court card, to represent the questioner. I feel that since we contain within ourselves and our lives all aspects of every card, not only the Court ones, it is important to make an entirely unconscious selection with each reading. Thus the significant card in the first or key place will pinpoint the particular issue or focus of the reading as it affects the unique person asking the question.

The Tarot and the Pendulum

Pendulum dowsing is a way of extending the scope of your intuition and this can be a highly effective method of selecting Tarot cards. You can use a conventional crystal quartz on a chain although many people find that a key on a piece of cord, a plumb bob or a favourite pendant is equally effective.

I do not recommend dowsing for every occasion but if you are having problems understanding a reading or the questioner expresses doubts about its relevance, try this method.

- Collect the cards into a pile, shuffle them and place them in a circle, face down.
- Allow the questioner to hold the pendulum and ask him or her to pass it slowly, first anti-clockwise, over the cards, beginning in the 12 o'clock position.

- The pendulum should then be passed clockwise slowly over each card.
- Ask the questioner to indicate which card the pendulum is pulling downwards towards most strongly. The pendulum can be passed around the circle two or three times if the choice is not immediate.
- Take this first card and place it on the left nearest the questioner.
- Ask the questioner to select a second and then a third card from the circle and place them next to the first selected card.
- Ask the questioner to turn over the three cards and these will provide the key to the reading.

Usually it is not necessary to select any more cards but if the questioner wishes to do so, use the pendulum method until the required number of cards are selected.

Keeping a Tarot Journal

A Tarot journal is an effective way of building on your knowledge and insights, as well as recording the milestones pointed out in different readings. The ideal workbook is in a loose-leaf format so that you can revise card meanings and modify spreads over months and years. I have seen beautiful A4-sized leather covers into the spine of which you can insert blank pages.

Alternatively, keep two Tarot journals, one an ongoing note folder and the other a more permanent record of your discoveries. You will need sections for:

- **Card Meanings:** You may find that your initial impressions are constantly revised both by practice, by information on specific cards gained from the numerology and Kabbalah sections, from your psychic work and by other books. You may also revise your personal Tarot journey through life and the Court card personalities who affect your world.

- **Card Spreads:** Even with basic layouts you will soon find that, with practice, you are altering the meanings of specific positions and creating your own spreads.
- **Cards of the Day:** Keep a table or chart of these. You may also need space for significant events linked with them.
- **Specific Readings:** You will want to study your personal readings and the knowledge you gained, both at the time and as events unfold. It can also be valuable to record readings you gave for others, especially if you found a reading problematic, as weeks or even months down the road you may see your original interpretation confirmed.
- **Predictions:** For calendar spreads or any long-term predictive spreads, it is helpful to note the actual cards and your feelings about them, as it can be difficult weeks or months ahead to recall precise details.
- **Tarot and Psychic Development:** You will need sections for your Tarot meditations, astral and past life work, together with dates, as you may find the persona and images gleaned in one experience, or a guide you met, may continue to appear and dramas unfold over a series of sessions.
- **Tarot and Crystals:** Note your crystal Tarot readings and information about your crystals, especially any healing or magical attributes.
- **Tarot and Astrology:** Note the astrological associations of yourself, friends and family. Prepare a number of zodiacal charts on which to enter your data to trace the course of your personal celestial sphere over the astrological year.
- **Tarot and Kabbalah:** Note the alternative pathways you can take on different occasions between the spheres, as well as your own evolving understanding of the Tree of Life. A series of Tree diagrams prepared in advance will allow you to chart your developing spiritual path.
- **Tarot Rituals:** This is perhaps the most valuable and unique aspect of your Tarot journal to preserve the words you use and the actions you carry out as you create your own rites. You can also keep a list of incenses, oils and

The Zodiac symbol for Cancer

herbs that you have found particularly evocative for different kinds of work.

Using this Book

The early sections of this book focus on the Major Arcana which are the first twenty-two cards in the pack, the Court cards and the Number cards which make up the Minor Arcana, and the spreads – the layouts of cards. This will teach you, even as a beginner, all you need to know. Should you wish, you need only use these chapters as a basis for giving readings for yourself and others. There is also additional material on using the Tarot to explore relationships and to plan a personal life path, but these are aspects that, if you are new to the Tarot, you may wish to leave until you are a confident reader.

You can do perfectly good readings with the twenty-two Major cards and many people add the Number cards only if they want to explore an issue in greater detail. They may then add the Court cards if there are a number of dominant or difficult personalities connected with the question they wish to examine.

It may be helpful to work through the first chapters which concentrate on the meanings of the cards in order, dipping into the Spreads section to try out the cards as you learn them. The first Spread involves laying out three, six or nine cards chosen at random from the pack and using them to build up a complete picture. You can use this with any section of the pack and it will cover questions great and small. This basic format is one that I have used successfully for many years and prefer even to the most complex layout for getting to the heart of the matter.

The later sections add more information about individual card meanings, linking them to ancient systems such as astrology, numerology, the Kabbalah and crystals, as well as using the cards as a focus for personal psychic development and meditation. Each is self-contained and they can be read in any order. Since the Tarot is such a powerful form of divination, a chapter explores the predictive aspects and suggests ways of using the cards for discovering the best times for important encounters or decisions. Finally the book examines ways of developing your gifts as a clairvoyant for friends, family and acquaintances, and becoming a professional Tarot reader if you wish. There are sample readings throughout the book of people whose lives the Tarot has aided, whether to make an important decision or to acknowledge their own needs, hopes and fears.

Part 1

Tarot
Essentials

Chapter 1

The Major Arcana – a Journey of Self-Discovery

The Tarot is called the Arcana because it is said to teach truths through symbolic language older than any written records, a language carried in myth and song, and so enriched by successive generations. These symbols address the unconscious mind and the psyche and so operate not through logical thought but by allowing these inner images to speak.

The Major Arcana, the first twenty-two cards of a pack, are frequently used alone for divination, since they are the archetypal symbols of human experience. They can also be considered as the stages of a journey through life, marking different stages in self-discovery and awareness. So this section gives both traditional concepts about the individual cards and attempts to follow the strands of the Tarot as a personal life path.

Creative and Receptive Cards

Rather than seeing cards as male or female, it can be helpful to regard the Major Arcana in terms of **creative**, energetic, active cards or **receptive**, passive, accepting and waiting cards, in the sense of yang and yin or Jung's animus and anima. In a Major Arcana reading, since there are eleven of each kind, a reading may be predominantly creative or receptive – sometimes waiting can be as important as acting.

The Cards of Your
Inner Powers

THE FOOL.

THE FOOL: CREATIVE

The Fool is the first in the twenty-two cards of the Major Arcana and anything but foolish. Like the Joker in card games, he can do anything or be anyone and change the whole course of the game at a stroke. As Wordsworth said, he comes 'trailing clouds of glory'.

He is Jung's inner child, the essential self stripped of worldly trappings, the real person that integrates our competitive and caring sides. In alchemy he is the divine hermaphrodite, the offspring of the marriage of King Sol and Queen Luna, the beginning and the end of any journey if we regard life and time as cyclic. T. S. Eliot says in 'Little Gidding' in the *Four Quartets*:

> *The end of all our exploring*
> *Will be to arrive where we started and know*
> *the place for the first time.*

Especially when his number is Zero (see the Tarot and Numerology, Chapter 10), the Fool is the seed of all potential, boundless and therefore limitless in the possibilities that lie ahead.

In the Universal Waite pack, which is very similar to the original Rider Waite cards, he is accompanied by his dog, perhaps representing the instinctive ability to find the right track. He is travelling light, carrying the white rose, alchemical symbol of rebirth, and about to leap off a precipice. But this is not a leap into the dark – rather a leap into the light.

The Fool is the most important card in the pack because he is saying 'Trust your own intuition'. And when, at the end of the journey through the cards, this wisdom is refined and uncovered from your own as yet only half-explored psychic depths, this will be the soundest piece of advice of all, for you will be drawing on the tribal wisdom of all times and places, passed on through the genes of your ancestors, which the Fool carries in embryonic form. You already have the power of the Fool within you and with it the key not only to the Tarot but also to making your own fortune. But the negative aspect of following your intuition can mean giving up the security that keeps many of us tied into less than satisfactory situations. You may even end up hurting people who can't understand why you have to leave them behind.

The Fool in a reading indicates that a major decision must be made although there are no clear pointers as to the right answer. Trust yourself, take that leap into the dark and do not look back.

THE MAGICIAN.

THE MAGICIAN: CREATIVE

The Fool is not alone on the Soul Journey as he has the Shaman to guide him through both the underworlds of the psyche and the sky realms of the spirit. So the Fool begins to see that life has patterns and so, like the Alchemist's apprentice, begins to learn about the ancient elements – Earth, Air, Fire and Water – that make up all life (even his own nature's patterns). As the environment and his own elemental composition is revealed to him, so he becomes both student and master of it.

The Magician is the Master Alchemist, descendant of the Egyptian/Greek god Hermes (known to the Romans as Mercury). Hermes is credited with writing forty-two books on astronomy, astrology, arithmetic, geometry, medicine, music and magic, and bears the healing caduceus with its entwined serpents.

Just as Hermes carried messages between Heaven, Earth and the Underworld, so the Magician is the message bearer and channel for the divine spark.

The Magician has the suits of the four Minor Arcana on his table, representing the four elements from which the fifth, ether or spirit, is created. As Alchemist in the Universal Waite pack, he links the everyday sphere with the magical and spiritual world, and seeks the all-powerful philosopher's stone that can turn base metals into gold and perhaps holds the key to immortality.

The Magician provides the creative energy to put your plans into action. When he appears, versatility is vital, for the Magician is the card of 'now'. Something is bubbling up inside and you feel excited and eager for change. The only negative aspect is that Mercury was also god of thieves and so whether it is those around you or yourself who feels that the end justifies the means, it is vital not to let integrity slide.

THE HIGH PRIESTESS OR POPESS: RECEPTIVE

THE HIGH PRIESTESS

The High Priestess introduces the Fool to his inner world, as receptive balances creative and the Fool meets the anima side of his nature.

She takes her name from the legendary ninth century Pope Joan, a woman said to have disguised herself as a man so that she could be elected Pope. But she is also very much associated with the maiden and the virgin goddesses such as the Waxing Moon Greek Goddess Artemis or the Celtic Brigid in her maiden aspect, patroness of healers, poets and smiths. In some packs she is called Juno, wife of the Supreme Roman God Jupiter, as the abstract, wise feminine principle of divinity rather than the sensual Mother Goddess.

The High Priestess is frequently portrayed between two pillars of darkness and light or mercy and severity, with her crescent moon at her feet and behind her a veil leading to the unknown. In some packs she holds the sacred scroll of the Torah, the Tablets of the Law, the body of wisdom given to Moses.

She is Eve before her union with Adam, receiving the creative seed of the Magician. The Maiden then gives form to the creative spirit, which will be born to the Earthly Mother, the Empress. The High Priestess is sometimes called the Spiritual or Archetypal Mother of the Fool.

This card can apply equally to men and women for it

is one of the inner world, inner change and aloneness (not necessarily loneliness).

The High Priestess is 'the unique self', the unchanging person you have been in essence from a child and will always be. It is the card that does not fear but rejoices in our separateness from others (a separateness which is inevitable from the time we leave our mothers' wombs).

In a reading the High Priestess may appear in response to inner, rather than external, events. She is a reminder of your own priorities and search for meaning. Finding the High Priestess buried in yourself is identifying where spirituality has its temple. It is time to start thinking about what it is that makes you, not other people, happy.

The only negative aspect of the High Priestess appears when she forgets her alter ego, the Empress, and is unable to understand and tolerate the weaknesses, needs and uncertainties of others.

The Cards of External Power

THE EMPRESS.

THE EMPRESS: RECEPTIVE

So the sacred dance between creative and receptive continues, and the Empress represents that state when temporarily we overcome the alienation and are part of the Mother, either within the protective womb or in nurturing life within us.

This card of Birth is the antithesis of the Death card and offers the Fool the certainty that, whatever happens, he is not entirely alone. In the womb and his early nurturing the Fool has experienced the state of unity in earthly form that mirrors the eternal unity with the Godhead. In Birth he will begin to separate and in Death be reunited.

The Empress is Isis with the infant Horus, the Virgin Mary with baby Jesus, icon of fertility, abundance and unconditional love and giving.

She represents the Mother Goddess and Earth Mother typified by Ceres or Demeter, the Corn Goddess of the

Classics, Cerridwen of the Celts, Goddess of the Full Moon, or Frigg in the Norse legends, goddess of women, mothers and housewives. In many packs the Empress is portrayed surrounded by corn, fruit and flowers, and may be seen in the aspect of the early mother statues in the full flow of pregnancy. In the Universal Waite pack, she is especially fertile with the astrological sign of Venus on the white heart at her side.

The aspects of the Empress are not restricted to mothers or even women, but the principle of creative giving in us all, caring, nurturing, accepting others for what they are with weaknesses and faults and a source of fertility in every aspect of life.

The Empress assures you that your emotional or practical support is vital to those around you and that, whether among family, friends or even at work, your role is making a happy environment. Yet there is a negative side to the Empress: what starts out as giving out of pure love or friendship can end with exploitation so that you lose sight of your own needs and identity – back to the High Priestess (you will find more of this in Chapter 2).

THE EMPEROR: CREATIVE

As the Empress was the Fool's earthly mother, so the Emperor is the earthly father who, like Christ's father Joseph, cares for a son whose spiritual potential far outweighs his own. It may even be that the Magician is transformed into the Emperor by his union with the High Priestess and so is the actual rather than surrogate father of the Fool.

This symbol of power and supremacy is nevertheless only earthly and so, in the opinion of some scholars of ancient wisdom, it is the Emperor not the Fool who dies as the Hanged Man so that the Fool can become the new wiser ruler in line with the natural order of change and progression.

The Emperor is the card of earthly power that the Fool must confront, rebel against and then assimilate the most

THE EMPEROR.

positive aspects into himself so that he will be greater than the father. The Emperor is the ultimate authority figure before whom all bow, the All-Father of many traditions, Zeus in classical mythology, the Norse Odin, the Wise One or Woden in the Anglo-Saxon tradition.

He is pictured enthroned, often in battle dress, for he is the experienced warrior as well as leader of his people. In the Universal Waite pack, he sits on his throne ready for conflict with Aries, the ram carved on his throne, endowing him with the courage of Mars, God of War.

The Emperor says that it may be time for you to assert what you want and be prepared to give your all. For whether this involves fulfilling an ambition, a career move, a desire to change location or your entire lifestyle, you may have been hesitating because action may involve confrontation. But be brave and act now.

The Emperor is so positive that he is bound to have a strongly negative aspect. Although he is the giver of law and decisions, laws may not always be just and decisions are not always wise, so there can be a critical, bullying aspect, especially in an authority figure in our lives whom it may take courage to confront.

THE HIEROPHANT

THE HIEROPHANT: CREATIVE

As well as authority, the Fool must learn wisdom and the great body of acquired knowledge, written and oral, as well as the deeper wisdom of the Collective Unconscious, teachings that are beyond time and space. The Hierophant is the archetype of tradition of all kinds and accumulated spiritual wisdom. In the classics he is Saturn or the Saxon Seater, the God of Limitation and Fate. In some packs he is called Jupiter, the Roman name for Zeus, the great god of the Greeks. He mirrors the Emperor, his *alter ego*, but in knowledge rather than authority. His wisdom is that of conventional and learned insight, gained through application. He is the mediator, linking mortals with their Higher Self or Spirit (or, as some believe, angelic guides).

So that the Fool can learn his own place in the world,

he needs to listen to his inner voice in the figure of the Hermit whom he will meet later on the journey. The Hierophant is the archetypal 'still, small voice of calm', that must be approached by discriminating between what is of worth and what is the ego of others who claim spiritual authority.

The Hierophant says that for now you should follow the conventional path, seeking advice from those who are wise and not just self-important. The answer is there if you seek in the right place, whether in books, from experts or through meditation and listening to your Higher Self.

The only negative aspect is if you allow yourself to be ruled by the ghostly voices of authority figures from your past who may have offered only destructive criticism.

The Cards of Confronting Life

THE LOVERS.

THE LOVERS: CREATIVE

The Fool moves now to find his or her *alter ego* in an equal in an attempt to recapture the connection he last experienced in the womb, now through his sexual and spiritual alchemy. The lesson is to explore opposites and complements, and inherent in this card is choice, attraction and rejection. Within this card too is the concept of dualism, of two halves meeting as one: twin souls. This brings the question: can we find our twin soul and if so can or should we merge with another?

This card of Relationships features the innocent Adam and Eve before the Fall who did not need to hide their bodies. Later in the Universal Waite pack they are ensnared by the Devil but rise again at the Last Judgement card. In the Universal Waite pack, Venus, Goddess of Love, hovers above the Lovers, but in other packs Cupid appears or a third party offers a choice – either between partners or earthly and spiritual love. The Lovers are also associated with the Alchemical Sacred Marriage of King Sol and Queen Luna, coming together to form the Divine Hermaphrodite who may be seen dancing within the circle of elements in the last card – the World or Universe. Originally the Lovers were a family group with a child between them.

And so the Lovers talks not only of love matches but all relationships, and the choices and balance that must be maintained between different people and between the needs of self and a significant other. Questions involving relationships are one of the main reasons people consult the Tarot. The Lovers is a card where ideals meet reality, and many conflicts in love and relationships arise when the actual does not correspond with the dream. In a reading, this card may be promising new love or that a new relationship will blossom. However, it may equally talk of existing relationships at a time when they need attention or seem less than satisfactory, perhaps because of false expectations.

The negative aspect of this card appears when we are locked in roles which perhaps no longer apply – protective father, helpless child – and we can end up feeling trapped by those we love. If this is a problem then it may help to see the people with whom you are involved as separate individuals with virtues and faults, rather than as angels or demons.

THE CHARIOT: CREATIVE

The Chariot is the card of change and ultimately triumph, of 'choosing the route' and changing direction. For though the Fool has found love, it is not enough and the world beckons to be explored and mastered. This card speaks of travelling, no longer as the footloose Fool, but as the soldier or explorer with a mission.

Apollo the Sun God rode his golden chariot across the sky so that the day might progress; Mars, God of War, steered his fiery chariot into battle; conquering Roman generals would return to Rome for their 'triumph', the victory procession through the streets in which they would drive their chariots, crowned with laurels. Whether black and white horses or sphinxes pull the chariot, the

Chariot card indicates that the rider has harnessed opposing powers to give the impetus to succeed, balancing the inner and outer worlds, the soul and body, self and other, but also questing further, like the Grail knights, to seek the answers and to find what will restore life to the barren land.

The charioteer will one day become the new Emperor. But he must be greater and combine the courage of the Emperor with the wisdom of the Hierophant, as well as the anima of the High Priestess and Empress so that he can dance at the still point of the turning world in the final card.

When the Chariot appears in a reading, it is a time for change, perhaps for travel, either actual or in exploring new avenues of life, for the first time within the constraints and yet concentrated motion of the Chariot. You need to balance all the aspects of your life, so that they provide the basis and the impetus for development, rather than walking away and starting over again.

The negative aspect of the Chariot is constantly changing the external circumstances when the problem is within, moving the old play to a new theatre with a different cast.

STRENGTH.

STRENGTH: RECEPTIVE

Strength may seem a strange card to be considered receptive. But it mirrors a gentle strength as found in the qualities of endurance, patience and persistence. The lesson that the Fool as charioteer learns is that in between setting out to the cheering crowds and returning in triumph lies the path to the Castle Perilous, many hardships, setbacks and obstacles that cannot be overcome by the force and courage of Mars, but by a different kind of courage.

Strength can be either card eight or eleven, depending on how your pack is numbered. But as this book is based on old traditions, I have retained the earlier position for Strength as Waite did (see also Chapter 11 on the Tarot and Numerology). Whatever numbering system you use will make no difference in a reading. In this card, also sometimes called Force or Fortitude, a woman is closing or opening the mouth of a lion. She is Cyrene, a maiden of Artemis, the Waxing Moon Goddess, whom Apollo the Sun God saw fighting and winning a battle against a lion. As a reward he took her to the realm of the gods.

Other packs depict Heracles (or Hercules) wrestling with a lion. He was unable to overcome the lion with arrows but eventually strangled it. Thereafter he wore the lion skin which endowed him with the strength and courage of the lion.

The woman is sometimes seen as the anima, the female magician, and in some packs she has a magician's hat but not his wand, showing that a personal, gentler approach can be more effective than brute aggression. This is the essence of the positive aspects of the Strength card. Sometimes persuasion, compromise and just sticking out a situation or course of action can be more effective than dramatic actions or walking away from less than ideal cirumstances.

In a reading Strength talks of life as it is, sometimes mundane or hard, and shows that by weathering a situation out, whether a rocky patch in a relationship or an apparently unrecognised period of effort at work, you can win through.

The negative side of Strength is sticking in a no-win situation, pouring energy and time into someone or something that can never come good. This is a time to use your strength for yourself.

The Cards of Reacting to Fate

THE HERMIT: RECEPTIVE

The Fool redresses the balance once more; having overcome the obstacles that occupied his energies through quiet strength, he looks inwards, making contact with the inner voice and withdrawing from the outer world of achievement to develop spiritual potential. It is a waiting time. The Hermit is the silent wanderer, standing apart

THE HERMIT.

from the world and its accolades, looking inwards into the depths of the ocean of the Collective Unconscious. He is the earthly form of the Hierophant, the connection between the personal inner voice and the 'still, small voice of calm'.

In the Universal Waite pack, the Hermit is seen as a seeker after enlightenment with his lantern. The Hermit is identified as Hermes Trismegistus, the semi-mythological patron saint of alchemy. According to the old texts, Hermes Trismegistus, thrice Great-Hermes, held within himself 'three parts of the wisdom of the whole world'.

The Hermit is the card of our inner voice and wisdom, the wise man and, for some, this wisdom may involve occult knowledge or formal spiritual paths. But for the majority of us it is a far more personal process of awareness. Ultimately the path of the Hermit is a lonely one, whether for inner enlightenment or withdrawing from frantic activity and the need to achieve to a state of just being.

In a reading the Hermit may be a pointer that it is time to step back from the world and from the demands of others and give yourself time. Often the Hermit will appear if someone is acting as a peacemaker for other people's quarrels and becoming the target of the anger of both sides.

The negative side of the Hermit is in withdrawing and not using the time and space to grow stronger, but becoming defeated, depressed and ultimately not resolving the issues that prompted the original need to withdraw.

THE WHEEL OF FORTUNE: RECEPTIVE

The Wheel of Fortune is the ultimate card of receptivity as the Fool learns that he is not the Master of his Fate, but must work with whatever cards Fortune deals. Yet he is not a blind victim either (see Chapter 5), for his previous and present actions determine to some extent the path he treads. In the Buddhist philosophy the Wheel of Birth, Death and Rebirth is turned by man's own actions

WHEEL of FORTUNE.

in different incarnations, so this symbol retains an element of choice and responsibility.

What is more, the Fool, like all of us, has the choice of responding positively to Fate, maximising opportunities and turning obstacles into challenge. At the moment the Fool is bound to the relentless Wheel, but can learn how to step off it by learning from mistakes and finding the timeless place both in and out of time, in the final card of the Major Arcana, the World.

Here too is a reminder of the cycles of life and the Wheel of the Year as the seasons and the constellations symbolically rotate along with man's life. Indeed, it may also be regarded as the Sun Wheel.

The Wheel of Fortune varies in different packs, the question being who is turning the Wheel. It may be the blindfolded Goddess Fortuna, suggesting that man is subject to the whims of Fate. Others show the Egyptian jackal-headed God Anubis, Conductor of Dead Souls, or the Egyptian God Amon, Controller of Destiny and Life, who is linked with the Sun God.

The Sphinx at rest at the top of Waite's Wheel is a reminder that we can choose and change our destiny through insight into the causes of seemingly random events.

In a reading this card never predicts that either good or bad fortune will strike, but usually refers to either a fear of disaster, hope of fortune or some twist of fate that has occurred at the time of or just prior to the reading. When the Wheel card appears you may be feeling helpless. You may not have the power entirely to choose your course of action but there is always some room for manoeuvre, even in the most seemingly inflexible situations. If in doubt, it may be time to follow the Hermit and withdraw for a while until you feel able to make a decision or have the confidence to follow your intuition.

The negative side of the Wheel of Fortune comes when you allow other people, whether fortune teller or authority figure, to impose a fixed vision of the future.

JUSTICE: CREATIVE

The Fool first encounters this card while railing against the unfairness of Fate. Justice is sometimes pictured blindfolded, not because she is unseeing like Fortuna in the Wheel of Fortune card, but so that she will not be swayed by external appearances. Rather, she will weigh evidence impartially, as the Fool must do if he is to become Master of Fate.

According to the Egyptian tradition, after death a man's heart was weighed against the feather from the head of Ma'at, Goddess of Truth and Justice. If the scales balanced, then the heart was free from sin and the deceased might pass to the after-life.

Traditionally the Justice card is associated with litigation and official matters, but in practice it usually refers to principles that are either currently of importance or are being eroded.

In a reading the card says that you may be fighting for a principle that is central to your happiness, whether it is a cause dear to your heart, a fairer working environment or division of labour at home; you may have suffered the injustice of an unfair slur on your name or professional ability or a betrayal of trust, either recently or from the past. It is not a time to compromise, but to fight for what is important to you, however little support you may have.

The negative side of Justice is a tendency to repress minor injustices against you to keep the peace and to hold on to past wrongs that cannot be put right.

The Cards of Confronting Mortality

THE HANGED MAN: RECEPTIVE

The Hanged Man is in many ways the most profound card in the pack, linked with the voluntary sacrifice of the old King or Corn God, so that the new order can begin and fertility continue. I believe this is the Fool's

THE HANGED MAN.

initiation into the meaning of sacrifice, as his father the Emperor ritually dies so that the evolved and wiser son could take his place.

But many see the Fool as the Dying God, the mythological sacrifice. The willing sacrifice is a universal concept: the Norse God Odin hung on the World Tree for nine days, surrendering his will to the greater mysteries of Life and going to the brink of Death in the manner of shamanistic initiation ceremonies, so that he was spiritually reformed and born in spirit. Odin finally saw the runes beneath him and in reaching down for them found he was free. So letting go is perhaps a better way of thinking about the Hanged Man than sacrifice, unless you give up immediate advantage or comfort for future gain, whether physically or spiritually. It is not an intuitive leap like the Fool's but a deliberate decision based on experience and maybe a bit of disillusionment.

The Hanged Man may appear when you have reached a crossroads and you have to decide whether to give up security, certainty or a destructive habit, resulting in an immediate loss or the need for extra effort. Three months down the road you will realise that you made the right choice, but at the time it is not easy.

The negative side of the Hanged Man is you become addicted to sacrifice, even for the best of motives. Nothing is sadder than an elderly, embittered parent who rounds on his or her children and says: 'I gave up everything for you and now I've nothing.' Danger comes when the giving goes on long after it is needed and the other person, too, can get locked into destructive dependency.

DEATH: RECEPTIVE

Death is the card of natural change, that has the most evil, yet undeserved, reputation. It cannot be said often enough that *THERE IS ABSOLUTELY NO WAY THAT TURNING OVER THE DEATH CARD MEANS THAT YOU, OR ANYONE CLOSE TO YOU, IS GOING TO DIE.* Death is merely a reflection of an inner state that already exists, but which you may be ignoring

or resisting. As such its positive meaning far outweighs any negative connotations.

So, for the Fool, through the sacrifice in the Hanged Man either of himself or his father, comes rebirth, regeneration and renewal, the second birth into redemption and immortality. Death is sometimes portrayed as the medieval Grim Reaper with scythe, as a black skeleton, or as a knight in black armour with a skull revealed through the helmet. The Universal Waite pack shows Death about to strike down bishop, king, lovely maiden and a child who, unlike the others, is not afraid.

On the deepest level our mortality is something we ultimately need to confront and work through. But the Death card talks of the hundreds of little deaths, the microcosmic transitions that we must undergo if we are to move forward, the 'death' of each stage in our life. If we can face change with the calm courage and optimism of a child, movement can be positive rather than the end of the world (you will meet the child again in the Sun card).

The Death card does not mean that a sudden end will come to a part of your life – out of the blue and out of your control. It indicates that a natural change is already taking place, one which you might not yet be aware of or perhaps are trying to hold back. We should allow our sadness and memories to emerge and make time to take stock and even grieve before going on.

The negative aspect of Death shows itself when we do not recognise that it is time to let go either in a relationship or of our dreams. Possessiveness is often rooted in fear of being alone and sometimes it takes great courage to accept we are no longer the centre of someone's world.

TEMPERANCE: RECEPTIVE

Temperance is, in alchemical terms, the philosophical gold of enlightenment which is slowly distilled from undifferentiated matter and illusion. The Fool must acquire moderation so that the excesses of emotion and of cold logic – the euphoria when things go well and the black despair

TEMPERANCE.

when setbacks occur – are refined into more subtle emotions that are related to actual events and not anticipated future glories or past regrets. Only by living in the present can the Fool truly gain control over the future.

Waite pictures Temperance in angelic form, though some see her as Iris, Goddess of the Rainbow, who could pass between the Underworld, Earth and Heaven. The action of pouring water is a sign of the interaction between unconscious and conscious worlds that is vital for inner harmony.

Temperance talks about harmony and peace of mind by avoiding unnecessary confrontation and redressing any imbalance of stress in one area of your life by making positive steps in another.

This card may appear when you have been feeling anxious or irritated by matters or people you cannot change. Concentrate on people who make you feel good and your positive achievements and, for once, let tomorrow take care of itself.

The negative side of Temperance is keeping the peace at all costs. Sometimes a short-term truce has a very high price.

The Cards of Light and Darkness

THE DEVIL .

THE DEVIL: CREATIVE

The Devil is the card of our shadow side, to use Jung's terminology, and, like Death, is a card which makes people wary of the Tarot. But it has no power to summon up or draw evil to you. Rather than an external demon, it represents our negative side which we must acknowledge and conquer rather than blaming forces outside us.

Indeed, the Devil as a power to be eradicated is a Judeo-Christian concept. In contrast the Oriental and some Western philosophies see evil as the other pole of good and that gods of evil, such as Loki in the Norse tradition, were a necessary facet of creation. Unless the

Fool acknowledges the darkness within himself, he cannot release his inner light, but will people his world with angels and demons who are really projections of aspects of himself.

Incorporated in many of the demonic images, including Waite's stern image, is the goat-footed pagan Pan, the Horned God of Nature. He represents natural instincts, Freud's Id, that if unbridled would destroy humankind's civilised world. Nevertheless, as Freud recognised, the basic instincts are necessary for survival and procreation, and provide a source of root energy and drive necessary for action. Waite's Devil depicts the couple first seen as the Lovers, chained in this card to each other although they could escape (indeed, many of us know apparently destructive relationships that are fuelled by the mutual needs of those involved and we do sometimes contribute not only to the making but continuation of our own hell).

The negative side of the Devil appears when your confidence is at such a low ebb that you feel you deserve nothing more than unhappiness.

But the Devil is a very vital and positive card which represents a basic fact of human nature. Each of us has negative feelings but rather than a defect they can be an impetus for change if channelled against injustice or inertia.

The Devil may appear when pent-up anger is bubbling beneath the surface. Confront the cause of your suppressed negativity and release the energy into your life to regain control over your emotions.

THE TOWER: RECEPTIVE

The Fool is now ready to confront the issue of permanence and the cycle of creation/destruction and renewal at the heart of all existence. If the old forms become too restrictive, damming up necessary growth and progress, the breakdown may be tumultous. The Tower of Destruction, the card of liberation from restriction, is rent by fire and tempest in many Tarot packs and Waite has his

THE TOWER.

couple falling as lightning splits open the Tower, though their hands are spread to break the fall. In some packs it is called the Tower of Destruction or La Maison Dieu, which is not literally translated as the House of God but a corruption of Diefel, the biblical Tower of Babel.

The Tower of Babel was built by the descendants of Noah in an attempt to scale the heavens to avenge themselves on God for sending the Flood. As a punishment, God sent down a confusion of tongues and henceforward it was said that not only differences in language but in understanding caused discord among people. In fact, this was in itself a liberation so that diversity, not only of expression, but also of ideas could germinate to prevent stagnation.

Although in conventional readings the Tower is sometimes interpreted as disaster, if you look at the Tower as a prison or a blind alley, it becomes very positive. This card is not predicting disaster but saying perhaps that what you have seen as a setback may in fact be a chance to move forward.

If you get the Tower in a reading, the wind of change may be blowing fiercely through your life, bringing long-overdue renewal, whether in a relationship, your work or plans, or even in widening your range of vision to seek new opportunities.

The negative aspect of the Tower is rebuilding the same edifice under a different guise.

THE STAR.

THE STAR: CREATIVE

The Star is both the inner star of illumination and the Fool's guiding star and inspiration as he looks upwards and momentarily unites with the harmony of the spheres. For once the walls of the dark tower have been split open the stars are visible and the Fool, like the Star Maiden in the Waite pack, has no material trappings or old burdens to hold him to the Earth. Now he does not leap into the unknown, but rather follows a path that extends like a tunnel of light from Earth to Heaven, linking his mortal form and his cosmic immortal self.

Stars have been a symbol of promise and guidance for seekers in many cultures. For the Ancient Egyptians, the appearance of Sirius, the Dog Star, heralded the annual flooding of the Nile which brought fertility to the parched land. The Magi followed their star to Bethlehem.

As the unclad maiden in the card pours water on to the earth to nourish it, in the same way dreams and hopes are nourished by practical action. For although we are wishing on a star, those dreams most likely to come true are those that we make happen through our own efforts.

You may see the Star when you are starting to make plans. They may be very long term and very ambitious – but you are taking real and forceful steps towards a future you want.

The negative aspect of the Star resides in refusing to settle for less than perfection. Dreams have to be anchored in reality and may have to be realised in a small way at first, so that we reach the stars bit by bit rather than in a sudden leap.

The Cards of Dreaming and Doing

THE MOON.

THE MOON: RECEPTIVE

The Moon is Queen Luna to the Sun, King Sol, her silver to his gold, the power of dreams, of lunar intuitive insights and emotions as opposed to the conscious power and awareness of the Sun. In this card the Fool learns to explore his psychic nature that can be assessed through imagination and dreams, the sixth sense that extends from the five physical senses. It is the gentle transition to other dimensions that co-exist with the earthly dimension that helps the Fool to gain the power to move naturally in and out of time.

The Moon Goddess was worshipped from early times in her three aspects that reflected the life cycle of maiden, mother, wise woman, birth, fruition, death and then rebirth again, a cycle that is mirrored in the passing seasons. Artemis is the virgin goddess of the waxing moon, Selene, the mother goddess of the full moon, and Hecate is the Crone, hag of the night, embodying the wisdom of experience and an awareness of endings. So the dark of the Moon, when we cannot see it in the sky and must trust it will return, becomes the crescent and new life is reborn.

The wolves and dogs baying on some of the cards are a primitive call of nature. The crayfish crawling out of the water is one of the oldest surviving creatures and co-habited with the dinosaurs, so it is the envoy of timelessness. This, then, is a very special card, containing elements of many of the others.

The Moon suggests in a reading that the world of dreams, daydreams and imagination rightly seem more important than external events. Listen to your inner self. Allow yourself to daydream and explore your psychic abilities. We are more than creatures of the everyday world and so if you let your inner star guide you for a while then you will after a time approach life with a new understanding and serenity.

The Moon has a bad side only if it takes over and you don't go back to the world, or you imagine that there are easy paths and short cuts to success and happiness. This is reflected in Waite's card, for the Moon, with its soft glow, can also be the card of illusions.

THE SUN .

THE SUN: CREATIVE

The Sun is the card of clarity and attainment, the base metal that has been transformed into gold. The Fool now is the new Sun God, at his full height at noon, who will decline each night and in the waning year in accordance with the natural cycles. That was the message of the Moon card.

Sun Gods have a central role in many mythologies; the Egyptian Re who ferried the solar boat across the sky each day; Helios of the Greeks, who was regarded as the Sun himself and ascended the heavens in the morning in a chariot, drawn by winged snow-white horses and, in the evening, plunged into the ocean; Quetzalcoatl, the Aztec plumed serpent deity of the Sun.

The Sun will always rise again each morning with promise and so the Fool has learned to make the most of happiness without demanding any assurances that there will be no more darkness or sorrow. It is the card of pure energy, optimism, joy and success in the world's terms, the *alter ego* of the Moon. It speaks of developing your potential, all the untapped or undeveloped talents and unique gifts you have that, at whatever age, can still fulfil many of those dreams seen in the Star.

Waite's golden-haired child is the Divine Child or the Inner Child in us all, made from experience and welding together all the conflicts and opposites to make something new and greater. In the Waite card he or she is riding away from the wall of limitations, though of course they are also the foundations that assure success, based on the past and maybe the best of that Tower that fell down.

If you get the Sun in a reading, it may be a new opportunity has presented itself and you may doubt your own ability or you may suddenly feel the stirrings of life and optimism after a stagnant or dark period. Whatever the situation, seize the moment and enjoy it. The sun does not always shine so when you have those golden days, take advantage of them.

So how can the Sun ever have a negative application? Sunlight can be harsh and if it is too intense it can wither lands and burn people and animals. We are only just discovering the cost of sun-worshipping to extremes. It's sometimes tempting to ignore the consequences of achieving a goal at all costs.

The Cards of New Horizons

JUDGEMENT: RECEPTIVE

The Fool reaches the end of his path and answers the question he first asked about his own mortality and being alone. This card promises that there is rebirth and unity

with Divine power that overcomes the dread of being alone. Nature is reawakened and the Fool realises he is part of the world, not alienated from it or above it, as God or the Goddess, goodness and the life force are also within nature and in the Fool himself.

Judgement, the card of reconciliation and spiritual renewal, is often depicted in terms of the Last Judgement and Waite has the characters of Death, the Lovers and the Devil rising up without the need for the trappings of the World before St Michael, who is depicted blowing a golden trumpet restoring life.

Michael is the 'light-bringer'. Judgement says there is no external Devil to carry us to Hell and that we must judge ourselves. Judgement acknowledges our humanity; sometimes we do make errors of judgement or judge others unfairly. Equally there are times when we were unfairly judged. This is the touchstone card, the hard, dark stone against which we test our beliefs and values and those of others, so that we are free to set our own internal standards and not be held back by the fear of disapproval of others or the need for permission from others before we act.

Judgement may appear when you have been feeling regret over an old quarrel or a missed opportunity. If you can put the situation right, do so. If not, accept that you or others made a mistake but that life is never easy and generally we act for the best motives or out of desperation. This was first mentioned in the Justice card, but now comes into the light.

The negative aspect of Judgement is best summed up in the phrase 'against your better judgement' when logic and common sense are warning you not to rush ahead blindly; it's time to listen to your head and not your heart.

THE WORLD: CREATIVE

The World shows the four elements united in the centre by the fifth element, ether, or the philosopher's stone. In the centre dances the divine hermaphrodite, the union of King Sol and Queen Luna, the Sun and Moon. For in

THE WORLD.

the Fool the conscious and unconscious animus and anima, light and darkness, are integrated in the dancing figure.

As in the Moon card the Fool learned to step beyond time, now he can dance in and out of time at the hub of the Wheel of Fortune, no longer subject to its rotation as mind, body and spirit move in harmony. ROTA the Wheel has become TORA, wisdom and enlightenment, the key to the Tarot. The cosmic egg which contains the dancer is, in Waite's card, vibrant with living greenery, the laurel crown.

The World, the end of expanding horizons and limitless possibilities, is a card of movement, whether involving actual travel or being open to new perspectives and ideas. It uses the symbols of the four Evangelists, Matthew, Mark, Luke and John, which also represent the zodiac signs Aquarius, Leo, Taurus and Scorpio, that are themselves signs of the four elements of Air, Fire, Earth and Water that appear throughout the Tarot.

If you get the World in a reading, you may find that now, or in the near future, all the pieces of the jigsaw come together and you can see the whole picture. You know that although there may be a long way to go you are on the right track. Whether outwardly or inwardly, your horizons are expanding and whatever anyone else says you have the confidence to strive for what is the true prize and not compromise.

It's hard to find a negative side of the World; but sometimes we are being swept along by events and so involved in activity that we may feel that we are losing touch with the people that matter to us. If so, then take time just to be with those you love and get back in tune with your personal centre.

Beginning your Personal Tarot Story

Each of the cards reflects an aspect of ourselves or our lives. Here's how to begin to discover your own personal Tarot story.

- Place the Major Arcana cards clockwise in a circle in order, beginning with the Fool.
- Beginning with the Fool, let the images flow through your mind. Write, either in the first or third person, a story that you might tell to a child: how a young man or woman leaves his or her home and goes into the wilderness where he meets a magician or a shaman who enrols him as an apprentice. The youth meets next a wise woman or priestess who takes him to a temple and shows him the veil through which the entrance to the mysteries lies. She delivers him to a palace where he is adopted by the Emperor and Empress.
- You may spontaneously write dialogue, snatches of verse or draw sketches of knights, ladies and dragons. At each stage, pause and take up the story from the point of view of the new character, then return to the same scene through the eyes of the Fool. Only write a page or so each day and don't worry if you have a pause of weeks if your external world is busy.
- Create the circle each time you return to the story, and before you begin, read the story so far.
- If you use a loose-leaf folder or copy the story on to a word processor you can alter it or you may prefer to add new chapters. When you have completed the Fool's basic life path, you can use the story method to work through any conflicts or sudden choices – the cards offer the stage, backcloth and props against which any drama can be set. You may feel after a while that you identify with a different character, perhaps the High Priestess or even the Angel in Temperance.
- If so, start a new story from that character's perspective and let the new persona wander through the Tarot scene. If there is a gap or you cannot see the way the drama should unfold, pick three cards from the Minor Arcana including the Court cards and use them as a bridge.
- This story method goes back through our tribal memory to early myths and not only helps you to gain a deeper awareness of the complexities of your own nature, but also

offers a way to read the Tarot for others, by reading the cards as an unfolding story, that can overcome conscious blocks.

- You can create Tarot myths for those who are close to you, and if you let your intuition speak, you may find this a way of overcoming the preconceptions and attitudes we project on to others.

- If you have a lover or partner or a close relation or friend, work with him or her and select a character to represent him or her, weaving together a legend that may reveal the dreams and fears you hold about your relationship. This is possible even if the other person is not present.

Chapter 2

The Court Cards – the Key to Relationships

To some people – and I used to be one of them – the Court cards are the poor relations of the Major Arcana. When I began giving readings, I tended to regard them as a diversion, or at best cards that bridged the Major Arcana and the Minor. But over the last few years I have come to realise that they are the jewels of the Tarot, linking the archetypal Major cards and the building bricks of daily trends and events in the Minor Arcana with the real personalities about whom the readings are talking. What is more, they can be used separately to focus on relationship issues and to uncover aspects of your interactions with others that can explain why conflict or misunderstandings occur and how you can improve these relationships, both personal and business.

The Court Cards and the Elements

Carl Gustav Jung, the psychologist and psychotherapist who took a keen interest in all things occult though he did not directly write about the Tarot, was fascinated by the classical and medieval divisions of people into temperaments. Humankind was seen as made up of the four elements in different proportions, which explained predominant character types observed first by the Greeks. This tradition continued through Roman times to the

Middle Ages and the Tudor period. So Shakespeare could write of Henry V, knowing his audience would understand him perfectly, 'he is pure Air and Fire; and the dull elements of Earth and Water never appear in him'.

In his own age, Jung identified these four elements with four basic ways of human functioning: Earth with sensations; Air with thinking; Fire with intuition; and Water with feeling. He paired these as two sets of polarities: thinking/feeling and intuition/sensation. He also believed that all people have a predominant element, a secondary one and, most importantly, a shadow element, the opposite from our predominant element. This soul image, as he called the opposing element, was absent from the conscious life, but might emerge in dreams or the choice of a future partner who reflected the missing function. So the thinking, Air person, according to Jung's theory, has a Water or feeling soul-image; an intuitive, Fire person has an Earth or sensations soul-image; the feeling or Water person has a thinking or Air soul-image; and an Earth or sensations person has a Fire or intuitive soul-image.

Each of the Court cards, in a similar way to Jung's categorisation, has its predominant element, its secondary element and its shadow element. There has been a great deal of psychological research to further categorise these personality types and some people have tried to link these categories with Tarot Court cards. This can add helpful information in not only identifying the people or the aspects of ourselves the cards represent, but also point to hidden strengths and qualities that may make interactions easier. I have also added my own interpretations of these trends.

However, our predominant element type is not set in stone, although we may naturally veer towards, for example, a feeling or Water rather than a thinking or Air response in everyday interactions, as Jung and the ancients suggest; what is more we may find the opposite polarity harder to access.

At different times and even in different situations during the same period we may reflect different Court cards. Whether we are male or female, aged eighteen or eighty, the aspects inherent in all the cards can be necessary at different times. We all display the power of the King at times when we need to assert ourselves or to be strong. The nurturing aspect of the Queen can be as vital to men as to women in their relationships and in developing their intuitive side. Equally the Knight in us represents enthusiasm for a venture that makes us reckless of consequences and more concerned with ideas and ideals than actual people or situations. The Page can stand for the formulation of a new idea or relationship, or the 'Help, mum' syndrome where we look to others to bail us out.

Each has strengths and weaknesses. Since the whole point of magic and divination is to harness different strengths at the appropriate time, thereby increasing the overall potential for success and happiness, it can be useful to regard the elemental modes as potential ways of responding to a given situation. For example, the most logical or normally predominantly Air person may automatically switch into Water or feeling mode in a close relationship and, more importantly, may benefit from deliberately bringing into the fore this Water element at a time when tact and empathy are vital.

Defining the Court Cards

There are sixteen Court cards, four more than in the playing card deck, because the Jack takes on two aspects: the Page and the Knight. The Court cards can have different names such as Princess and Prince, Daughter and Son, and even Priestess and Shaman, instead of the traditional Queen and King, but most keep the traditional titles. These Court cards usually refer to personalities who are dominant or difficult in our lives or who represent aspects of our own personalities that are significant or needed at a particular time, as stages in personal development.

Identifying the Court Cards

There are two main ways of identifying specific Court cards: first by physical characteristics; then in considering the elemental nature of the Court card dealt and adding the mental and emotional characteristics to the outer person. But these physical characteristics are also only a framework. We all know a charismatic fifty-year-old Knight of Cups married to patient, capable Queen of Pentacles, whose ageing boyish charm catapults him from one chivalrous flirtation to another while she worries about the mortgage and unblocks the drains.

You can use either system of physical characteristics in different readings, although you may find that one system applies more naturally. For example if you have younger children you may identify them with the Page cards and the Knights with children who are grown up. But if you are, say, male and under thirty-five with a partner the same age you might see yourself in matters of love and Tarot love spells as a Knight and your girlfriend as a Page. In some packs the Pages are called Princesses, but even here you can use the child/teenager/young adult association if it seems more relevant to you.

THE PAGES

Predominant Mode: Sensations
Shadow Aspect: Intuition

The Pages are cards of the Earth and may refer to a child or younger teenager of either sex or an adult female under thirty-five. But if the person is not identified during a reading, the card can represent an undeveloped aspect of the questioner's personality as tentative ideas or dreams, or the first steps towards a new goal or relationship. So Pages can be very positive cards.

In the Universal Waite pack the Pages are all static figures in the open air, showing that at this stage all things are possible and the direction of the future is undecided.

On a more negative note, Pages can represent a person of any age who is childish.

PAGE of PENTACLES

The Page of Pentacles

Predominant Mode: Sensations
Secondary Mode: Thinking
Shadow Side: Intuition

By the Jungian definitions this is the archetypal Page, the child of the Earth who builds up a picture of the world through formative experiences, and what he or she hears, touches, tastes and smells.

The Page of Pentacles is pictured by Waite against a background of sunny skies and green fields, linking him very strongly with the land. The Page of Pentacles is a reliable, hard-working and studious young person who is loyal and stoical. What this Page lacks in excitement is made up in reliability. Living always in the real world, he or she is concerned more with doing than thinking and will usually comply externally with the arguments of others, afterwards going on his or her previously determined path. However, this Page can be unimaginative and unwilling to try new things.

If you get the Page of Pentacles, you may be glad to be able to rely on someone younger. Or you may be planning a simpler, perhaps slower way of life. If you keep your feet on the ground you can't go far wrong. On the other hand, you may find yourself in a practical or financial mess, apparently out of the blue, and your first reaction is to rely on others, rather than your own resources. It is time to call on logic and buried intuition.

If it is a younger woman, she will want security from a relationship, material as well as emotional, but will work tirelessly to build her nest.

The Page of Cups

Predominant Mode: Feeling
Secondary Mode: Sensations
Shadow Side: Thinking

Because he is a Page of Cups, the feeling aspect takes precedence and emotions can affect both physical well-being and functioning.

PAGE of CUPS.

The Page of Cups is a dreamer, kind, sympathetic, easily hurt and sensitive to the needs of others. Waite's card emphasises the Water element with a fish emerging from a cup. The soft colours and flowers on his tunic suggest the gentle, intuitive nature of Cups. So the Page of Cups is a creature of gentle contemplation, of sentiment rather than high romance and passion, of dreams and daydreams rather than flashes of inspiration. He or she will idealise people, especially those seen as more experienced and wiser. This Page will be blind to faults and so can easily be betrayed, also unworldly and unable to accept criticism. Getting in touch with what is really happening (sensations) and using buried logic will help.

The Page of Cups can turn up when you are looking for friendship rather than high romance and need to take your time in any relationship, or when your dreams are important in helping you through a mundane or difficult patch, although here you must be careful not to spend so much time dreaming that you miss the real thing.

If this Page is a younger woman, she will follow her lover anywhere and live in a tent if necessary, but will expect high standards of fidelity in return.

The Page of Wands

Predominant Mode: Intuition
Secondary Mode: Thinking
Shadow Side: Sensations

PAGE of WANDS.

The Page of Wands is quite complex and, in his or her natural *modus operandi*, sensations get buried beneath all the inspiration and new ideas. He or she can be seen to be the least materialistic Page.

The Page of Wands is the original free spirit, quick-witted, curious, imaginative and eager to try anything new. His or her ideals are untainted by the desire for success and enthusiasm for life is unbounded. This Page is the child of Fire in a desert setting with the symbols of the salamander (the legendary fire lizard) on his tunic. He stands for the innocent idealism and enthusiasm for life that we all begin with but which, sadly, sometimes gets lost and replaced with cynicism. This is a very special Page, idealistic and artistic in the widest sense, reminding us of things we once held dear and that lie half-forgotten inside us, buried by the years.

However, the Page of Wands is easily distracted and can be volatile, swinging from elation to depression at the first sign of difficulty. The natural connection with the Earth inherent in Pages should be rediscovered and logic applied to the actual situation and not just abstract ideas.

If you get the Page of Wands it may be that a child or younger person is to gladden your heart with their ideals and enthusiasm. The card can also represent a half-formed idea that, as yet, lives only in your head but may have great implications in the future.

If this Page is a young woman she will be highly independent and always want a career, but will be supportive of those she loves in sickness and health.

The Page of Swords

Predominant Mode: Thinking
Secondary Mode: Sensations
Shadow Side: Feeling

PAGE of SWORDS.

This is the most determined and rigid Page, the old head on young shoulders who worries endlessly about everything from the environment to the interest rate on his or her savings.

The Page of Swords is clever, observant, humorous and aware even at a young age of life's limitations and injustices. He or she seems to symbolise aggression but his sword is thrust out in defence not attack. The birds and butterflies around him, Air symbols, soften the logic and thrust of the Swords and his dominating force is fear. This fear, which may be unfounded, is holding him back from enjoying the blue sky and nature around him, and causing him to act in a hostile manner. This uncertainty can make him or her seem devious and careless of others' feelings.

However, he is also skilled at manipulating facts and using whatever is at hand to achieve his ends – for good or ill. But the goodness if coaxed out will be a potent force against inertia and injustice. So he or she needs to learn to empathise with others from an early age and not despise those less capable.

The Page of Swords may appear when someone is masking their insecurity with aggression and needs kindness and reassurance. It is a hard card to deal with because our natural response to an attack is to be hostile in return. But understanding will pay dividends.

You may be hesitating at the beginning of a new venture because of the memory of past hurt and failures. Put the past behind you and one day soon you will be ready for that new beginning.

As a younger woman, this Page may have experienced sorrow early in life and so is less trusting; but once she finds someone or something worthy of faith, she will make any personal sacrifice for her loved ones.

THE KNIGHTS
Predominant Mode: Intuition
Shadow Side: Sensation

I had until very recently regarded the Knights as the cards of Air and this is an accepted viewpoint, also one I had used in my earlier book *Tarot* (Piatkus, 1999). However, throughout magical practice, Air and Fire are subject to a certain amount of interchangeability depending on which tradition is followed. If one accepts the Jungian concept of personality types it would seem that the inspirational aspects of Fire are closer to the Knights than the Kings, the other correspondence.

The fiery Knights have far more movement than the Pages and reflect the initial enthusiasm and passion of new relationships and ventures. Knights are either older teenagers or men under thirty-five. A Knight can also be a partner or friend of either sex who is adult but still free from responsibility or perhaps not fully mature.

If the Knight in a reading is not identified, he or she may be part of a new facet of the questioner which is emerging to act out of character or to take up a cause. The negative aspect is the immature person of any age who pursues his or her own desires at the expense of others.

The Knights are the heralds of news in the area of the next card in a reading. Above all, they are a reminder that the world can be an exciting action-packed place if we take our courage and cast aside those conventions that restrict us.

The Knight of Pentacles

Predominant Mode: Sensations
Secondary Mode: Feeling
Shadow Side: Intuition

KNIGHT of PENTACLES.

The least knight-like of the crusaders, the natural mode of operating intuition can be buried in this Knight and he or she can have a real problem rebelling as he is aware of the effect his actions have on others.

The Knight of Pentacles is the most stable of the knights, tempering restlessness and crusading with a strong vein of reality and a respect for the world. He is the most likely to succeed, because he never forgets the consequences of his actions. The reason he may not be galloping his horse is because he is in a cultivated field. He is the conservationist, a respecter of tradition who will not be afraid to work hard and with little reward for a worthwhile cause.

The challenging aspect is that this Knight may lack the vision to explore wider horizons and so he needs to allow his innate intuitiveness to emerge, perhaps through the channel of his feelings.

The Knight of Pentacles may stand for someone you

know whom, although not old in years, does have an awareness of life and others, yet retains enthusiasm and beliefs. If the card is reflecting a facet of you, then you are probably well on course to succeed in whatever venture you are undertaking, as long as you continue to combine common sense with a worthwhile cause.

As a male under the age of thirty-five, this Knight will be the dutiful relation, the patient and undemanding lover who will do his utmost to please and may be puzzled by a lack of response.

The Knight of Cups

Predominant mode: Feeling
Secondary Mode: Intuition
Shadow Side: Thinking

KNIGHT of CUPS.

The Knight of Cups is the original Knight in shining armour. He or she offers excitement, sentiment and romance and his or her quest is for perfection in others – as well as self. The Waite Knight moves slowly on his white charger carrying his Grail Cup, looking for and prepared to sacrifice all for love.

He or she is the poet, the musician, the seeker of beauty of spirit as well as the flesh. Facts are of less importance than what is of worth.

The negative aspect of this Knight is shallowness of feelings and inconstancy in affections, partly caused by finding that the idol is human. This is where logic and clarity of vision should be called from the buried psyche to find happiness in the real world.

If you meet the Knight of Cups then your life will not be short of excitement, sentiment and romance. Prepare to be flattered and adored – if you can keep this Knight at your side. If the Knight is a part of you then you may still be looking for your ideal partner or a fulfilling friendship rather than settling for second best. But do not miss the chance of happiness by constantly scanning the next horizon.

If this represents a male under the age of thirty-five, he will be the perfect lover and defender of the weak, once his roving eye is firmly fixed in one direction.

KNIGHT of WANDS.

The Knight of Wands

Predominant Mode: Intuition
Secondary Mode: Feeling
Shadow Side: Sensations

The archetypal Knight of legend, the Knight of Wands follows the path perilous without regard for personal hardship or danger.

The Knight of Wands is the great communicator, creator and inspiration for others, the innovator who devises brilliant schemes and loves travel and risk of any kind. His armour blazoned with salamanders, he rides at full pace for God and King Harry or whatever happens to be the current good cause. This Knight represents perpetual motion and impatience with the speed at which life progresses in the everyday world. Once he or she gets started, there's no stopping. The negative aspect is a tendency to flit from one project to the next, completing nothing. He or she can also be liberal with the truth – and so a dose of reality from the Shadow Aspect would not come amiss. Nor would increasing awareness that he may be hurting others' feelings – which would horrify this Knight who is basically very caring.

If you encounter the Knight of Wands, you are about to enter life in the fast lane – either under your own steam or propelled by someone close to you. It may also be a time to push through personal projects and to channel your enthusiasm into creative ventures and to fulfilling your potential, so long as you are not diverted.

If this is a man under thirty-five, any lover will have to compete with personal organiser, mobile phone and a portable computer, even in the bedroom. But if you share a cause or dream then there is no stopping the relationship.

KNIGHT of SWORDS .

The Knight of Swords

Predominant Mode: Thinking
Secondary Mode: Intuition
Shadow Side: Feeling

Logic and the purging aspect of the Fire element ensure that this Knight will have great impact on all he or she touches – for good or ill.

The Knight of Swords has perhaps the most impetus and determination of all, challenging injustice and showing courage against the most powerful odds. Waite shows him charging into battle, the tempest blowing round him. His will is like the steel of Swords and he will plan any action like a military operation. The negative aspect is obsessiveness and a willingness to sacrifice others for his cause.

The Knight of Swords in your life may be off into battle, leaving you on the sidelines hoping that he won't get hurt. He may also trample over the feelings of others if they get in the way and this is where the intuition and inspiration of the Knights can help him to imagine how he would feel if similarly treated and so curb this tendency. As a personal quality, the Knight of Swords may turn up when you may feel that you can no longer ignore repeated provocation. But be sure of your facts before you charge and be certain that you are not letting anger run away with you.

As a man under thirty-five the Knight of Swords will have built up many barriers or never been emotionally awakened. But with patience he will learn to show gentleness and care.

THE QUEENS

Predominant Mode: Feeling
Shadow Side: Thinking

The Queens, the Water Element, represent a more mature woman, whether a mother or a female authority figure, symbolising female fertility and wisdom. If there is no

Queen whom you recognise, the card may stand for your own nurturing side. The Queens apply not just to women, but to the anima, the caring, gentle, receptive side of every male. They are very positive, creative cards and often appear with the Empress, emphasising a particular aspect. The Queen is the pivot of many people's worlds. The key to understanding the Queens is discovering what keeps her on that particular throne; necessity or choice?

The negative aspect is in possessiveness or living other people's lives for them.

The Queen of Pentacles

Predominant Mode: Sensations
Secondary Mode: Feeling
Shadow Side: Intuition

In this Queen feelings are sublimated in practical actions that can stifle the imaginative, intuitive side.

The Queen of Pentacles, sometimes called the Queen of Hearth and Home, is a woman (or man) who deals with practical and financial affairs in such a way as to make all around her comfortable and secure. She is the carer of the sick, the old and the troubled, not by dispensing advice but with practical help. In the Universal Waite pack she is surrounded by fruits and the richness of nature, suggesting she has much to give. She is the Queen whose home we all love to visit, especially if we are feeling in need of tender, loving care.

The negative aspect is that she can become obsessed with order or take over the responsibilities of others and become a martyr. In this case the feeling and intuitive aspects should be used to explore her own feelings – negative as well as positive. She must decide if she is expressing her own need to be cared for when she rushes around fulfilling other people's every need – and whether this emotional drain is dulling her creative powers.

The Queen of Pentacles points to someone close to you who provides the security and comfort. Or you may

QUEEN₀ꜰPENTACLES

be caring for family, friends or colleagues, whether at work or home, in practical ways and are central to the well-being of others.

The card warns that you may end up providing the practical or financial back-up for all those Pages who call for help every time a problem looms. Do we encourage other people to rely on us because otherwise we would feel redundant?

QUEEN of CUPS.

The Queen of Cups

Predominant Mode: Feeling
Secondary Mode: Sensations
Shadow Side: Thinking

This is the archetypal Queen who gives love, support and approval to all through every aspect of her being and, if upset, will feel and sometimes become, like the vulnerable Page of Cups, ill in mind, body and soul.

The Queen of Cups is naturally intuitive and peace-loving, totally in tune with the feelings of others and the natural world. She represents fertility and creativity in their widest sense. Her challenging aspect is in emotional possessiveness and in seeking ideal rather than real relationships. Here is the universal agony aunt on her watery throne, surrounded by mermaids and contemplating her particular Grail which holds all manner of wisdom. She is the ever-smiling peacemaker between friends, relatives and work colleagues. But others tend to project their own hidden traits on to her. This can mean that the expectations placed upon her are overwhelming, and she needs to take time to summon that buried logic and be aware when the body is giving warning it is becoming over-stressed.

It is hard to find drawbacks to the Queen of Cups, although in a real crisis, it's too easy for her to take over too many responsibilities which are other people's, letting them off the hook, and occasionally getting emotional satisfaction through other people's relationships, rather than her own.

The Queen of Wands

Predominant Mode: Intuition
Secondary Mode: Feeling
Shadow Side: Sensations

Don't expect tea or sympathy from this Queen; her enthusiasm is for ideas, causes and for helping people to find solutions to their problems rather than letting them wait for her to do it.

The Queen of Wands is the wise woman, independent, authoritative but also intuitive and imaginative. She is at the hub of activities with her enthusiasm and ability to weld together disparate people and interests, but she does not live through her family, though she may be happily married and a mother.

She is sometimes wrongly labelled the Queen of Hearth and Home for her black cat is a symbol of magic, not domesticity, and she has the sunflower and the lion to remind of her links with the Fire. She is probably a natural healer and an ace Tarot reader.

Her negative aspect is in her impatience with those who seem weak or lack vision and her inability to let others take the lead. She needs to get in touch with her five senses so she can see what is actually happening and hear what is being said, not what her fast mind is filtering to fit in with preconceptions and theories.

The card appears when you, or someone close to you, is at the centre of organising schemes that affect those around you. You know that although life can get frantic with all the conflicting demands on your time, you are achieving positive results.

The Queen of Swords

Predominant Mode: Thinking
Secondary Mode: Sensations
Shadow Side: Feeling

There but for the grace of God goes a betrayed Queen of Cups with her predominant mode and shadow side reversed.

QUEEN of SWORDS.

The Queen of Swords is the disappointed woman, whether in relationships or the workplace, whose own past or present sorrows can make her bitter and over-critical. The love and kindness still exist beneath the surface and she may prove an unexpected and powerful ally in adversity. Her challenging aspect is her inability to express love and gratitude, and in being unforgiving, so seeming insensitive to the feelings of others.

In Waite's card she sits on her throne amid darkening skies holding her sword almost as a ceremonial object. She is sometimes associated with divorce, widowhood and even illness, but whether she is someone close or part of you, her key is responsibility and caring in times of difficulty for she is the Queen of sad times, either her own or those she loves. Given someone who will empathise with her sorrows and worries, she may discover those long-buried feelings.

You may get the Queen of Swords when you want to protect someone who is unhappy or in difficulty but you know that going into battle on their behalf won't help and you must wait until they ask. Don't underestimate the support your presence gives.

Even the negative side of the Queen of Swords is not malicious. Perhaps out of desperation or sheer unhappiness, the Queen is tempted to resort to emotional blackmail when she should be letting go of a no-win relationship.

THE KINGS

Predominant Mode: Thinking
Shadow Side: Sensations

The Kings represent mature or older men or male authority figures. They embody power, achievement, paternalism, justice, wisdom and responsibility. They are the Sky Fathers of ancient tradition and represent Air in its most potent and positive aspects, clear communication, learning, logic and the ability to cut through inertia and injustice.

If you do not recognise the King in your reading, he

may represent your own animus – your desire and drive to succeed. This can give us a boost if we are wondering whether or not to go ahead with a plan. These cards of the Air element talk of power and responsibility and like the Queens can refer to male or female, young or old. Some people automatically associate a King with their father or boss or husband just as they see the Queen as a mother figure.

The Kings' challenging aspects are domineering ways and inflexibility.

The King of Pentacles

Predominant Mode: Sensations
Secondary Mode: Thinking
Shadow Side: Intuition

In this King maturity has integrated the aspects of his personality. Thinking is normally the shadow side of sensations, but here it has become the secondary mode, at the cost of free-thinking (intuition). Sensations too are refined so that they represent success in material terms through focused application of the five senses.

The King of Pentacles has succeeded either financially, in business or in a practical, methodical way and is firmly rooted in his domestic world of which he sees himself as benign Lord and Master. He works hard for family or to make a comfortable base and is honest and generous. He is the friendly bank manager, the honest estate agent or wise older person who tempers experience with compassion. His negative aspects are that he can be over-cautious, obsessed by detail and materialistic or so involved in work that he forgets those for whom he is working. This is not through lack of feeling, but a narrowing of focus and the re-emergence of intuition may bring this King back in touch with the other important side of the personality.

This card indicates concern with security and achievement in worldly terms. There is nothing wrong with wanting the best for ourselves and those we care for and in sticking at a goal. The card says it is important to be single-minded, watch financial matters closely and pay attention to detail to ensure long-term prosperity.

KING of CUPS.

The King of Cups
Predominant Mode: Feeling
Secondary Mode: Intuition
Shadow Side: Thinking

In this King the natural power of the King is in shadow and so he may find his role as a King at odds with his emotions, although his intuitive strengths are well integrated so that he wins power by inspiring others as well as winning their love.

The King of Cups is the most approachable of the Kings. Popular and benign, he puts people above property or achievement. The Universal Waite's King sits safe from the stormy seas around him, for his inner world is as important as the outer one. He may be spiritual, religious or involved in the caring professions, but is invariably the dreamer who believes in the goodness of humanity to the end of his days and is constantly striving for perfection. At his best, this is a card where family and partners can feel secure because the King is happiest supporting and protecting those he loves.

Because he is aware of other people's feelings and rules by consent, thereby finding disapproval hard, he is easily depressed and this can render him impotent to make decisions or even stand against injustice. For this reason the thinking function needs to be developed so that his judgement is impartial and he does not play favourites, as this can make him a difficult person to work for.

His negative aspects are sudden bursts of anger and flirtatiousness because of his lifelong struggle for ideal love.

This King may appear when you are contemplating a serious commitment. If there's a choice between permanent love or excitement, between the King or Knight of

Cups, opt for mature love. Or you may know this King and worry about money and his non-competitive attitude; value his caring qualities, but make sure he does not spend so long helping others that he forgets those closest to his heart. If you are the King, you may have a burning desire to help others and should follow your heart.

The King of Wands

KING of WANDS

Predominant Mode: Intuition
Secondary Mode: Thinking
Shadow Side: Sensations

Logic and inspiration make a powerful combination and so this is probably the most effective King, although the least practical in responding to the here and now.

The King of Wands is a man of vision and ideals, a natural entrepreneur, persuasive, an expert communicator and driving force behind many ventures, energetic, optimistic and eager to share his considerable knowledge and wisdom. He lives life to the full and expects others to do the same, loves travel and may move house frequently. This is the card of career and ambition to succeed in whatever field.

Waite's King of Wands leans forward on his throne, his salamander beside him, ready to leap into any breach, carrying through plans no one else would even contemplate, and always full of energy and optimism.

His negative aspects are selfishness and lack of long-term commitment. But this is mainly where the thinking function has been swamped by the creative and so these two functions need to be kept in balance. An awareness of the world of external perceptions rather than hypotheses and possibilities will ground this King so that his creativity has tangible results.

If you get the King of Wands in a reading, then achievement in a chosen field is your driving force or that of your particular King of Wands. It's a time to be assertive and overcome opposition or inertia in others by energy and enthusiasm.

KING of SWORDS.

The King of Swords

Predominant Mode: Thinking
Secondary Mode: Sensations
Shadow Side: Feeling

The King of Swords is Archetypal King at his most positive, but because his secondary mode is sensations, the desire for dominance can sometimes swamp his natural desire for justice, especially as feelings are well buried. The King of Swords may appear totally rigid and lacking sympathy with humanity, but his strength is in his powerful sense of responsibility and in using logic and clear thought to succeed. This King is associated with authority figures such as government officials, judges, lawyers and doctors, both men and women.

Waite's King of Swords is surrounded by symbols of prosperity but the storm clouds are looming. Like the Queen of Swords, he is holding the sword ceremonially, the sword of justice rather than of aggression.

His negative aspects are pedentary and calculated cruelty to opponents. But for those he loves he will lay down his life. The development of feelings, which may have been blunted by earlier sorrows, will refine the sensations so that he empathises with the effects of any actions.

The King of Swords says it's time to be determined and cool-headed and make judgements based on clear thought and not emotion. If you are living with a King of Swords whose constant criticism is destroying your confidence, you should fight back with logic and refuse to be browbeaten. Most Kings of Swords will back down if challenged.

A Court Card Reading with the Jungian Spread

This method of reading is inspired by Jung's theory of the archetypes, the ideal figures that we carry within us, such as the wise father and the good mother which we can find represented in the Major Arcana. It is especially useful for looking at relationships or sorting out why you keep finding yourself in the same position. If you can look at the unconscious influences on you, the voices of these ideal characters in your head, it's often easier to see the best way forward. You may find it helpful to look at the predominant, secondary and shadow aspects of each of the cards, especially if one seems unclear, but as this spread incorporates those aspects in its overall form, I have not concentrated on them specifically.

Try your Jungian Spread with the sixteen Court cards alone, the Major Arcana or, perhaps best of all, the sixteen Court cards and the Major Arcana. It does not work well with Minor Arcana cards alone. Deal as usual, placing Card 1 in the centre of the table.

Now make a square surrounding the first card, dealing clockwise so that Card 2 is directly above Card 1, Card 3 is to the right of it, Card 4 below and Card 5 to the left of Card 1.

Place the cards face down, but turn over each one and read it before revealing the next card.

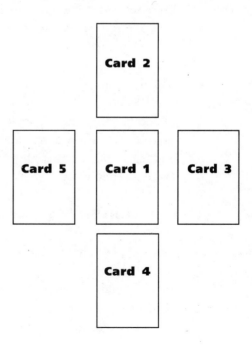

Card 1 is your *key* or *predominant pattern* card. This represents the predominant issue that is influencing you, not for all time but perhaps over the last few days or weeks. You may even have noticed it in your dreams. It may be a person or a particular issue or a pattern of reacting to certain situations or people that is causing problems in your life.

Card 2 is your *animus* card, the way your competitive, assertive, masculine, logical side or maybe the forceful argument of others, are, at this point in time, affecting your life and decisions. Don't be surprised if a Queen or Page turns up here – you may be finding it hard to get tough or people may be bringing emotional issues to cloud what should be a head not a heart aspect.

Card 3 is your *anima* card, the caring, nurturing receptive side of your nature or the influence of nurturing, mothering people that may either be helpful or smothering. A Knight or King in this position suggests a conflict of interest forcing you to hide this gentler side, perhaps if work is particularly hard or competitive or everyone is depending on you.

Card 4 is the card of your *shadow side*, the hidden fears or hostilities in yourself or your life. This area is an important aspect of the personality and negative feelings channelled in the right way can give strong impetus for change and success.

Completing the circle round Card 1, is **Card 5**, the *Inner Child*, the real essential you, what you really want and feel, whether on a physical or spiritual level, free from the expectations and demands of others.

TRISHA'S JUNGIAN SPREAD

Frank and Trisha have been married for three years and both have children from their first marriages, although Frank's children are much older and have school-age children of their own.

Trisha recently took early retirement from her job as

an administrator and Frank says that she should work in his shop to save him staff costs and spend more time with her step-grandchildren. Trisha feels pressurised as she would like to take a degree at the local university as a mature student, but Frank says it is a waste of time at her age. Now she feels guilty and selfish.

Card 1, the *key card* or *predominant pattern*, is the Queen of Swords which represents Trisha feeling like the bad fairy. But she has brought up her own children who are living abroad and does not want to get involved as more than a friendly visitor with Frank's children. Her efforts with the step-grandchildren have been rejected, since Frank's grandchildren are very close to their mother and their grandparents and regard Trisha as an intruder.

Card 2, represents the *animus*, the logical, assertive side of Trisha. The Knight of Wands says that Trisha should fulfil her ambitions, as money is not a problem. Trisha has a good pension, Frank's shop is doing well and he can afford to pay for assistance.

Card 3, the *anima*, the caring, nurturing side, is another Court card, the Queen of Wands, saying that Trisha can best express affection for Frank's family if she has an independent life and so does not make emotional demands of them. Frank is desperate to play happy families, although he himself has not been close to his children for years. She has been wife and mother for many years and if she allows herself to be manipulated emotionally, she may find that her loving feelings become tainted by bitterness.

Card 4, the *shadow side*, is the part of ourselves we keep hidden because we think other people won't like the true person behind the constant smile. Trisha deals the Devil himself and so should express her own negative feelings, rather than absorbing those of others.

Card 5, the real Trisha, the *Inner Child*, was another revelation: the King of Wands, hidden ambition that needs to be expressed if she is to become herself and not just a reflection of how others see her.

The Jungian Spread is not one for choosing between options but is valuable in unravelling thoughts, feelings and the roles we play consciously or unconsciously. Because it is such an intimate spread, it is one primarily for quiet evenings with trusted friends or, if you do read professionally for a client, after several sessions have established a deep rapport.

The Gypsy Love Card Spread

Sometimes used with playing cards, this is one of the old Romany spreads that involves the whole pack. Any Court cards that appear are of great significance.

THE METHOD

Shuffle the cards and lay out three face down. Turn the cards over from left to right. Then lay out a second and a third row, each of three cards.

Row 1: The Cards of your Relationships

These first three cards concern your current or projected relationship as it is now, and any questions or doubts you may have. Now lay three cards immediately below this row.

Row 2: The Cards of Outside Influences

These talk about the influences of others on a relationship or potential relationship, whether opposition or pressures to marry, have children, etc. Turn them over and read them one at a time, then see how they fit together. Now choose three more cards and place them face down below Row 2.

Row 3: The Cards of Suggested Action

The final three cards offer the way forward. Turn them over and read them one at a time and finally see your whole reading as a picture that has built up.

THE SUITS AND RELATIONSHIPS

If one suit predominates in this reading then that suit may represent the key issue in your life at this moment. If, for example, there is a predominance of Cups or Pentacles, you may find that emotion in the first case or practicality in the second, is swamping the relationship. Look especially at the row where they predominate. If there is a preponderance of Wands in the row of outside influences, it may be that you are being pressurised by other people's dreams. If Swords dominate, you may be being forced by others to consider major issues before you are ready.

Pentacles talk about the practical issues in a relationship that if unresolved can lead to conflict. These include questions of money, security and domestic arrangements, all of which can chip away at romance and passion. For example, while a woman feels resentful about doing most of the housework, her partner may equally object to spending every Sunday with her mother.

Cups deal with the emotions, with passion, loyalty, jealousy, resentments, trust and emotional blackmail. Often this is an area where outside influences can cause the most problems since parents, children and friends can all have emotional stakes that may conflict with the needs of a couple.

Wands talk about communication in love; all those ideas and dreams a couple may have that are just as important as sex and sentiment. Communication can so easily get lost amidst the practicalities of life, or worse still become muddied by past failures and fears of rejection that can make lovers see criticism and unfair comparison where none is intended.

Spades are not about bad luck but represent the challenges and changes imposed by fate and fortune. Some of these challenges involve decisions arising from the natural development in a relationship: when to live together, whether to have a family, whether to continue a career or stay at home with young children, move house, care for elderly relations or when to plan retirement. Or they can involve an unexpected pregnancy, promotion or illness that can seem to herald an ending but in fact can offer new opportunities and a whole new path.

Fitting the Court Cards into your World

List each of the Court cards in your Tarot journal and link them with people in your immediate sphere or as facets of your personality or people who are important to you.

- Concentrate on the positive aspects and see how the negative side can be turned into strengths.
- You might find it useful to record these impressions and see how they change over the months.
- You may find that you occupy more than one card role, according to the relationship and situation.
- Note, too, who you would like to be – many a Queen of Pentacles is an embryo Queen or even King of Wands.
- When you meet someone new, see which Court card they most resemble and the card in which their reactions cast you.
- Subtly change your own card and see how that brings about a change in others.

Chapter 3

The Minor Arcana – a Map Through Life

Each component of the Tarot is of importance both as a separate unit and in providing a different level of experience. These combine to make the Tarot a powerful tool of divination, spiritual development and a practical guide to daily life. As you move through the archetypal images of the Major Arcana and the personalities of the Court cards to the myriad examples of everyday situations, dilemmas and resolutions in the Minor Arcana, so the cards in a sense become more specific. For this reason I suggested in the introduction to this book that you selected two cards each morning, one a Major Arcana card to show you the underlying influences and then one from the full Minor Arcana, Court and Number cards, to tune into the personalities and the predominant trend each day.

But just as you can read the Major Arcana cards on their own, you can also read the Minor Arcana separately. The Minor Arcana can home in on specific issues and everyday problems. Since a quarter of the pack is made up of the Major Arcana, you would expect three Minor cards (including the Court cards) for every Major card dealt. If you get a higher proportion of Major Arcana cards, traditionally it's said that fate or outside influences have the stronger hand. It can also indicate that the issue under question is a central one and that we may need to take a long-term view.

A predominance of Minor cards can indicate that you

have more choice. It can also point to either one or a number of smaller specific issues and suggest that it may be helpful to concentrate on a short-term plan.

Reading the Tarot Suits

Each suit refers to a particular aspect of experience. If you get mainly one suit as opposed to a mixture of suits in your card readings, then it may suggest that this sphere is one that is troubling you or is especially vital right now though you may not have acknowledged it.

PENTACLES

Pentacles or Discs correspond to the element of Earth and symbolise the Communion dish from which Jesus ate the paschal lamb. In Celtic tradition it represented the ancient Stone of Fal, on which the High Kings of Ireland stood to be crowned (see Chapter 11 on the Tarot and Magic).

Pentacles are closely linked with the attribute called sensations by Jung, the five senses and above all common sense. They refer to the everyday practicalities of life, financial matters, prosperity, physical and material security, property, legal and official matters, the home, family, the qualities of patience, caution, perseverance and placidity, children and animals. They promise firm foundations for any venture.

You may get mainly Pentacles when you are working for a long-term goal and have faced many setbacks. The cards of Pentacles can offer hope that all your efforts will bear fruit if you persist. You may be in a job or home situation where you will need to put in a lot of practical effort and pay scrupulous attention to detail, but the material results will make your step-by-step progress worth while. Children, animals and all who are vulnerable may need your extra care.

On the negative front, you may be doing too much and feeling overwhelmed with all you have to do. The answer is to refuse to take on the burdens of those who are capable of managing their own lives and to delegate. Care for yourself as you do others.

CUPS

Cups or Chalices are linked to the element of Water and symbolise the Grail cup from which Jesus drank at the Last Supper, and the ever-full Celtic Cauldron of the Dagda (see Chapter 11 on the Tarot and Magic).

They correspond to the attribute Jung called feeling, empathy, sympathy and a response from the heart not the head. They refer to love, emotions, relationships, fertility, healing, especially emotions, peace and reconciliation with others, sensitivity, adaptability and gentleness, and the world of dreams and psychic awareness, to people in their twenties and thirties, and all who are in love, whatever their age.

If you get mainly Cups in a reading, there may be a commitment of the heart in the offing, a new stage in a love relationship that may involve adjustment or some hidden or unacknowledged turmoil with family, close friends or colleagues in which you may need to act as peacemaker. Or it may be that you feel very strongly about an issue or have a burning desire to follow a new course.

Do what you feel and not what you think, whether love or the valuable instinctive feelings that so often are the best guide to people or situations. Opening your heart to those you love right now is the path to happiness. If in doubt follow your heart and, like water, go with the flow.

On the negative front, you may be overwhelmed by the emotions of others. Resist emotional pressures and appeals to sentimentality.

WANDS

Wands or Staves are linked with Fire and symbolise the sacred lance that pierced Jesus' side and in Celtic tradition it is the magical spear of the young Solar deity, Lugh.

Fire corresponds with the attribute Jung called intuition, the inspired solution, the inner voice and inner promptings that draw upon the wisdom of our ancestors, the Tribal Voice that is passed on in our genes.

Wands represent creativity, originality and individuality, personal happiness, beginnings, communication and all artistic ventures, the world of ideas, of energy, excitement, action, ambition, success, career, health, travel, expansion, business partnerships, communication, mature people, business partners or colleagues.

A predominance of Wands indicates that your world is full of movement and that if you can focus on a particular goal or find a new solution to an old problem, you will achieve happiness and fulfilment. It is a time to act independently and to concentrate on personal goals.

The negative aspect of Wands is an inability to persevere when the initial enthusiasm has worn off and to take on more new projects than you can possibly handle.

SWORDS

Swords are linked with Air and symbolise the Sword of David, instrument of Justice and, in Celtic tradition, the undefeatable sword of Nuada of the Silver Hand.

Air corresponds with the attribute Jung called thinking, the power of logic and rational deduction, and so Swords is the suit of reason, courage, determination and calculation. Swords are unfairly regarded as an unlucky suit because they often appear after or during difficulty. But they represent the power to cut through barriers and initiate necessary change. They also stand for limitations, challenges, tradition, formal learning, justice formal and informal, and assessment, older people and ageing.

In a reading a predominance of Swords says it is time for the head, not the heart, to apply the reality principle and to cut through illusion, red tape and doubts to focus on whatever must be done; then carry through the task single-mindedly without hesitation. Swords say that we start from where we are and not where we would like to be.

The negative aspect of Swords is a tendency to allow inner fears or past failures to stand in the way of moving forward. The message time and again in these cards is that reality is never as bad as our fears.

Interpreting the Numbers

The Universal Waite Minor Arcana is so clearly illustrated that you can give any card your own interpretation just by looking at the picture. Many other packs follow these interpretations and even cards that use only the suit symbols may use the Waite meanings in the manual. Numerological meanings are also a good indicator (see Chapter 10 on the Tarot and Numerology in this book and also my *Complete Guide to Divination*, Piatkus, 1998 for an explanation of numerology). If you turn up the following numbers of each kind, note these indicators:

- four of the same number means an extreme result, whether joy or sorrow;
- three of the same kind is an indicator of the harmony of different forces;
- two of the same kind can demonstrate, according to the suit, either a conflict of interest, a reconciliation or new connection.

THE ACES
The number One is ruled by the Morning Sun and is the ultimate beginning and end, source of all energy. So Tarot Aces are vital and very exciting cards, whatever the suit, because our lives are full of new beginnings – from the first day at school to a life in retirement – and the Aces tell us to meet each challenge with all the energy and enthusiasm of the original Creative One. The chance to start again, especially after a traumatic change, and the

belief that the sun will rise again and tomorrow is another day can be the only things that give us hope during the darkest of nights.

When you get an Ace of whatever suit you know that new opportunities or an unexpected change of plan or attitude are on the horizon.

The Ace of Pentacles

ACE of PENTACLES

The Universal Waite pack shows the Pentacle being offered by a hand from a cloud above a carefully cultivated garden. So the ideal above is translated into action and the tangible result manifest in the garden. For since Pentacles are the element of Earth the Ace involves a new beginning in a practical sphere and promises that success or fulfilment are within our grasp if we are prepared to make that step-by-step effort and not look for instant rewards.

The Ace of Pentacles, like all Aces, speaks in a reading of change but on a material or practical level. You may need to change your job or learn a new skill to adapt to the changing world. There may be a change of home or a new home-related project or an upsurge in prosperity.

The negative aspect is when you are too burdened with practical concerns and miss the new opportunity.

The Ace of Cups

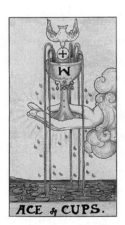

ACE of CUPS.

In the Universal Waite pack a hand raises the Golden Cup from the Waters. The dove of spirituality and peace above the Chalice links this card with the Holy Grail legends and the Lady of the Lake. So from the deep waters of the psyche comes the cup of fertility that will restore life to the parched land.

The Ace of Cups is almost always a joyous card, representing a new beginning in the world of emotions, either a new relationship or friendship, a new stage in a relationship or the beginning of a more spiritual path; the stirrings of trust after betrayal. It can also indicate conception or the birth of a baby.

Its only negative aspect appears when we let others

force the pace or expect instant fulfilment. Occasionally it can signify unrequited love.

The Ace of Wands

In the Universal Waite pack this is the magic wand of myth and fairy tale, symbolising new growth and energy, for the Ace of Wands as the first card in the suit of Fire is the most dynamic. It is a living wand, with leaves and buds, perhaps cut as by magicians of old from the hazel tree of wisdom or the healing and oracular ash.

It can signify a new beginning in career or improvement in job prospects, a new ambition, original ideas, a new perspective or opportunity to travel, a return to health, a new channel of communication; a desire for independence from a restricting situation or a burst of energy to clear stagnation. It is the card of pure inspiration and so is a very exciting one to turn over whether you long to be an artist, a poet, a communicator, an inventor or just to find personal happiness.

Its negative aspect is in translating the ideas into practical action and not being deterred by the lack of enthusiasm or vision of those around you.

The Ace of Swords

This is the first card of the suit of Air and is a double-edged sword. Perhaps, for this reason, the Crown unites the olive branch of peace and the palm symbolising victory that lies at the end of a difficult road after a bitter and painful battle, shown by the shed leaves.

In readings, this card heralds a beginning under difficult circumstances. But it is also a powerful, positive card of change, and offers you the courage to see any obstacles as catalysts for new directions, using your head rather than your heart which may have left you vulnerable in the past.

The only negative aspect of this card is if you let past bitterness, however justifiable, sour the new start.

THE TWOS

These deal with partnership issues, both in love and business and with balancing events or resolving disparate demands on our time. The Creative One has split into the Two of Duality and Diversity and is ruled by the Waxing Moon (see Chapter 10 on the Tarot and Numerology). In it exist the polarities of light and darkness, good and bad, masculine and feminine, competitive and nurturing, but with the positive energies of increase inherent in the growing lunar disc. The Twos can either indicate the problem of trying to juggle two balls that keep flying in opposite directions or the harmony of two people dancing in step.

So in a reading it can be a number of union or division, of double the strength or the splitting of power and resources in opposite directions.

The Two of Pentacles

This card talks about juggling the practical calls that are made upon us; the logistics of balancing work and home or different people with equally demanding needs. The Universal Waite card shows a young man successfully balancing and juggling two pentacles. However, the rough sea behind is a reminder that all may not be as smooth as it seems on the surface.

The Two of Pentacles in a reading may indicate that there are two major strands in your life that are of equal importance or that you yourself are developing in two different but complementary directions that for now must balance. It may also suggest coming together with another person for a mutually beneficial venture, improved domestic arrangements or an extra source of income.

The negative aspect is when you feel pressurised by the weight of practical commitments and demands on your time. You may need to decide what are your priorities and to delegate if you are not to become exhausted.

The Two of Cups

Here the relationship aspect is predominant and Waite concentrates on the harmonious union of a couple drinking a cup in celebration and perhaps as a pledge. The two serpents of good and evil are entwined around Hermes' healing caduceus, a reminder that real harmony is the positive awareness of union of all aspects of the self and other, rather than seeing a two-dimensional ideal.

The Two of Cups may herald the deepening of a relationship, whether love or friendship, a firm commitment of love, marriage, mending of a quarrel or a period of harmony, also the coming together of two different aspects of life or people who may not have seen eye to eye in the past.

On the negative side it can be the card of conflict, where choices are demanded between two family members or between a partner and parent, partner and child or in a work dispute. You should not be drawn into the quarrels of others as they may both blame you.

The Two of Wands

This is the card of alternatives. Waite gives quite a gloomy interpretation, talking of Alexander the Great's sadness amid the grandeur of this world's wealth. The man pictured in the Waite pack stands between two wands from the safety of the battlements, looking over the sea and mountains. It is unusually static for Wands and says that sometimes you do need to wait before acting so that you can be certain you are taking the right course.

The Two of Wands may appear in a reading when the question in a career or life generally is whether to strike out alone and if you do move on, to where? Plans involving others may seem temporarily restrictive and a business partnership or work relationship may need approaching with care if it is to bear fruit in the future, so unusually for Wands, this card counsels patience.

The negative aspect is the problem of balancing job or personal life and health where exhaustion or stress may be a factor.

The Two of Swords

The blindfolded woman of the Universal Waite pack or the woman hiding her eyes is a common motif of the Swords. Here she sits almost ritually between crossed swords, behind her the uncharted waters of the psyche, frozen by fear.

The Two of Swords in a reading says that a choice must be made even if neither option seems promising. Use logic and independently verified facts where there may be conflict between two people or aspects of life or to decide which of two conflicting pieces of information is true.

The negative aspect is to continue to do nothing and allow Fate or others to make your decisions.

THE THREES

Threes are thought to have great significance as the number of mind, body and spirit, and the Holy Trinity and in alchemy where King Sol and Queen Luna (the symbols of One and Two) have produced the divine child that is greater than them. The number Three is said to be ruled by Jupiter. Therefore the cards of Three have a strong creative element and represent the achievement of initial goals and hope that whatever has been gained is a sure foundation for future success.

A Three in a reading speaks of short-term results in your efforts, so enjoy or accept what is happening now in the knowledge that change will follow.

The Three of Pentacles

The Universal Waite pack shows the partial completion of a structure and is an assurance that efforts you have put in have not been wasted and that working with others rather than alone is now the key to success.

The Three of Pentacles says any venture you are undertaking does have firm foundations. Like the Three of Cups, this card may herald a birth or addition to the family, although a Pentacles addition is often by marriage or an elderly relation rather than an infant, also extra commitment or responsibilities that will prove of long-term advantage.

The negative aspect of this card appears when you take on extra practical burdens out of necessity or obligation that may weigh heavy at a time when you are already heavily committed.

The Three of Cups

Universal Waite shows three women dancing around, in Waite's words 'pledging each other'. The fruit and flowers, symbols of fertility, strengthen the concept of a celebration, whether a marriage or birth or reconciliation or meeting after an absence.

In a reading the card promises a period of emotional happiness with family, friends and loved ones, so take time now to enjoy it as such moments do not last for ever.

On the negative side, however, the card may indicate rivalry in love or friendship; emotional conflicts where two people are seeking sympathy or favour from a third. Stress can be caused by other people's emotional pressures and blackmail.

The Three of Wands

The man we saw in the Two of Wands, standing on the battlements looking out, has moved on to stake a claim in the future and marked out his path with his three staves. This can indicate that a plan has been made or a step forward taken, whether towards independence or personal fulfilment.

In a reading the Three of Wands says decisions about travel and moves of all kinds are in the air. Take your time planning; business or work commitments and opportunities may increase and will demand extra energy and input; communication may involve several people.

The negative aspect is an awareness that the way ahead may be a lonely one even if you are in the midst of a family, for others may not be willing to follow.

The Three of Swords

The Universal Waite card shows a heart pierced by three swords with the rain lashing and storm clouds gathering. But in fact it talks about the triumph of logic and reason over emotion.

The Three of Swords may turn up in a reading when you have been on the receiving end of malice, rivalry or emotional blackmail. Success and happiness lie in keeping your head and ignoring any petty spite or gossip, however much it hurts.

The negative aspect is being forced to make painful choices and acknowledging that perhaps a seeming friend is in fact causing trouble for you with others.

THE FOURS

The Fours are the cards of organisation and stability, the real world with its limitations that can seem stultifying or reassuring. They are the cards of security.

These cards are said to be ruled by the Evening Sun (or in some systems Uranus, the planet of change and originality. See my book *Tarot* (Piatkus, 1999) for an alternative version) as the power of the Sun moves closer to the Earth. Four represents the earthing or grounding of mind, body and spirit within the material plane (the triangle becomes a square).

The Four cards represent the conflict between accepting what we are and what we have as opposed to the unknown, the exciting, the desire to hold ourselves back where we know it is safe. Many of the limitations we impose on our lives are through fear of change and the unknown.

The Four of Pentacles

This is the card of holding on to what has been partially achieved or attained in a practical or material sense. We may be afraid that if we carry on with a new course of action, we may fail and lose what we have gained so far. The Universal Waite character is unable to move, because if he does he may drop what he already has.

You may turn up the Four of Pentacles if you are considering a practical change in your domestic or financial life or in matters regarding children that involve risks and you fear that if it all goes wrong you will be worse off materially. But, in the words of another old maxim, 'you have to speculate to accumulate' and you must decide whether the danger of stagnating is greater than the risk of losing what you have.

The negative aspect of this card is that you may be experiencing limitations financially, perhaps connected with property, and so the loss would be disastrous, which makes a decision hard.

The Four of Cups

The Universal Waite shows a young man sitting beneath a tree with three cups. A fourth is being offered by a magical hand (perhaps the one that held the Ace of Cups). But he has to reach out to take the cup. We all reach the point in a relationship where we need to make a decision to commit or trust or to move back.

If you get the Four of Cups you may be experiencing general feelings of restlessness and emotional dissatisfaction and your own or another person's commitment may be under question. It's perhaps time to share your fears with the other person involved to discover if the doubts are justifiable.

The negative aspect is giving in to a free-floating desire for something more exciting, the pursuit of which may put at risk a worthwhile existing relationship or friendship.

The Four of Wands

The Four of Wands represents success and recognition of achievement, but prompts the question 'What is the next stage?', for there is an inner restlessness that will not be contented for long.

The garlanded Waite hero is riding into the fortified manorial home in victory.

In a reading this card represents success and achievement personally or career wise and provides a good basis for future achievement, especially in creative fields.

The only danger is if the security aspect becomes imprisoning and you do not move on to fulfil your ultimate goal.

The Four of Swords

This shows the effigy of a knight with swords hanging above him and one on the tomb and the intimations here are of the ghosts in our head, the fears that may seem very real and which can paralyse us into inaction.

The Four of Swords in a reading indicates that limitations and obstacles come mainly from inner fears based on past disappointment, failure or betrayal. Examine these fears in the cold light of day to make them disappear.

The negative aspect of this card is the inability to write off old injustices and cut your losses, however great. If you cannot do this, you will remain the prisoner of the spectres of the past.

THE FIVES

These are said to be ruled by the planet Mercury and so are linked with both communication and versatility. The traditional instability of the Tarot Fives reflects this quicksilver quality that at best can encourage us to question a stagnant or redundant situation and communicate our needs and fears, and at the worst to abandon what we have worked so hard to create.

The Five of Pentacles

Two beggars in the snow find the lighted church window above offers them no comfort. The conventional sources which might help the needy in a practical way are inside the church praying.

In a reading the Five of Pentacles may appear when temporary practical or monetary obstacles create a feeling of isolation. This card tells you to look for a new source of help or advice, maybe from someone you might not have thought of in the past as particularly friendly or understanding. Plans should not be abandoned but modified; building on what has been achieved.

The negative aspect of this card is not letting people see what you really need, especially if you are normally a tower of strength and perhaps not getting the support you deserve at your moment of need.

The Five of Cups

The man in the black cloak sees only the three cups that are spilled and not the two remaining. The Five of Cups reflects misunderstandings in relationships, disappointment perhaps after an initial honeymoon period when reality sets in, or there is a sudden quarrel or cooling of affection.

In a reading this cards says that it is important not to give up as our dissatisfaction is only temporary. There is still a reservoir of goodwill or love remaining. Speak from the heart as lack of communication may be the problem.

The negative aspect of this card is giving way to temptations and passions which may not, in the long term, bring happiness. Heed the warning of the card and look at the two full cups not the three empty ones.

The Five of Wands

The Universal Waite card shows five youths fighting with staves. In the midst of a struggle you may need to be extra assertive over personal plans or projects at work. Make sure you get the credit for your input and ideas. This testing time is to be welcomed as you will emerge stronger and the ideas that survive are guaranteed success.

On the negative front, care should be taken to avoid accidents through tiredness and carelessness, as well as stress from over-involvement in problems caused by others. Rivals may be less than open in communication.

The Five of Swords

A fighter has beaten off the opposition. He holds three swords and two lie on the ground. The traditional interpretation assumes that the card reader is represented by one of those in retreat and often advice is offered to accept your limitations. On the other hand, the card may be saying that success lies in using the other aspect of the Swords – logic – to defeat apparently overwhelming opposition.

In a reading the Five of Swords says that since your cause is just you should continue to fight, as you are holding your ground, in spite of the odds against you.

The negative aspect warns you to beware of hidden spite and less than honest dealings by others. You may need to be less open about your intentions.

THE SIXES

The Sixes are ruled by Venus and reflect peace and harmony and events that turn out better than expected. However, Venus also brings an element of escapism and idealism. The Sixes mirror, not only outer calm, but also an inner peace or need for it because sometimes the Tarot can show us what we desire as well as the current situation.

The Six of Pentacles

This is a progression from the miser of the Four of Pentacles and talks of the balance of giving and receiving practical help. Unlike the Five of Pentacles, you may be the one giving and that can be very creative and satisfying as long as you remember also to give to yourself.

If you select the Six of Pentacles in a reading, pay attention to documents and details, especially in contracts and official papers. Keep a cautious rein on finances and avoid taking on too many commitments. This is a time for reflection and conserving energy rather than action. Family matters may take up time, but these can be immensely rewarding.

The negative aspect is in consistently giving out rather

more than you are getting back financially or in practical assistance.

The Six of Cups

The Universal Waite pack shows children, cottages with roses around the door and flower-filled cups, making it a card rooted in the past. It is a card of harmony and contentment and perhaps returning to your roots.

In a reading the Six of Cups is the card of nostalgia in the nicest way, with joy and satisfaction coming from family affairs, children, older people, animals and perhaps reviving old relationships or friendships that have been lost or weakened by time. It may not be too late to rekindle the past.

There may also be a reconciliation, especially with older people.

The negative aspect of the Six of Cups may appear when you are waxing sentimental about old times. Perhaps it really was as good as you remember – or maybe today's relationships are proving less than harmonious and you want to turn the clock back so that the old romance and magic return. In fact, the only way you'll get them back is by making happiness right now, taking what was good about past relationships, minus the rose-tinted spectacles, and using it to rekindle present joys.

The Six of Wands

The Six of Wands heralds promotion or recognition of your worth and says that you are on the right path and should not doubt yourself. The victor is riding crowned with laurels to the cheers of the admiring crowd. Your idea or gamble or personal path has proved to be the right one, even if approval is more muted than that shown in the card. You will, in the near future, have your efforts rewarded or at least acknowledged.

If you get the Six of Wands in a reading then it's a clear pointer that you have got the balance right between achieving your own happiness and not hurting others, between work and personal affairs. So you can go ahead with confidence, knowing that this is the first of many small victories on the way to finding happiness.

The negative aspect is the temptation to rest on your laurels.

The Six of Swords

The Six of Swords says that calmer times are ahead after a period of unrest or uncertainty, so long as you leave behind any bitterness or regrets. This card is sometimes taken to indicate travel but more often it signifies that you need to move forward in some aspect of your life.

The boatman in the Universal Waite card is taking the female passenger into calmer waters. But this does not mean that you can settle back and enjoy the ride and wait for better times to come. The woman is obviously leaving after some setback and the boat starts off in stormy waters.

If you get the Six of Swords it is time to stop worrying over old troubles or fighting a lost cause and, instead, move forward. The important thing is to seek your own peace of mind and that may mean accepting that some injustices cannot be put right and you may not get compensation for wrongs done to you. Brooding over past troubles is the negative aspect of this card.

THE SEVENS

The Sevens deal with wisdom acquired through experience. These cards are ruled by the Waning Moon, as people withdraw into their inner world. In some systems Seven is ruled by Neptune (see *Tarot*, Piatkus, 1999), but the qualities are not very different. Seven is the most spiritual and mysterious number and is found in many religious symbols. So the Sevens deal also with our unconscious wisdom and the search for something more than material success. There may be a hint of illusion, for it is a number of dreams and imagination – but dreams can be the first step to finding happiness.

The Seven of Pentacles

The Seven of Pentacles in the Universal Waite pack shows a young man resting while collecting the harvest of Pentacles; but he has not finished his task. Like the Six of Wands it is a card indicating rest or respite and perhaps a reassessment of the next step, trusting, unusually for Pentacles, your intuition.

The card may appear after a period of hard work or worry about money when you are feeling tired and wondering whether you will ever finish what seems a monumental task. It is a time to take a few days off or go on a holiday if you can; then your enthusiasm and energy will return. Long-term material security is augured, for this is the card of the harvest.

The negative aspect is doubting the point of your endeavour, but feeling unable to step off the wheel even temporarily.

The Seven of Cups

The Universal Waite card shows a young man hesitating over the choices of wealth, security, love, danger and the unknown element. The Seven of Cups involves the need to choose between several options or paths, between success in the world's terms or emotional satisfaction.

In a reading, you may be at a crossroads. It may be necessary to consider the less certain path where emotional and spiritual fulfilment offers less tangible rewards.

The negative aspect is in indecision or the illusion that we can have it all.

The Seven of Wands

This card carries a certain amount of controversy over its precise meaning. Some see in the Universal Waite card a youth defending himself against six other wands, the opposition to his ideas and ideals. Waite himself emphasises that the youth has the vantage position and the other wands attack from below. Others see the young man uprooting his stave and setting himself apart from the

crowd. But both interpretations are not that far apart. Ideals are important and there may be principles for which you need to fight; ultimate happiness comes from seeing beyond immediate returns to a long-term goal.

The Seven of Wands may appear when you are finding it hard to stand by your principles or live with people who have very different values. So it's quite a lonely card, but also very positive, for you know that ultimately there's more to life than the approval of others.

The negative aspect is, in defence, descending to the level of those with less vision and integrity.

The Seven of Swords

A man is making off with five of the swords and looking very guilty as he does so. The Seven of Swords warns that there may be less than honest behaviour among those around you, with gossip and petty spite.

It could be that someone close to you is claiming part of the credit due to you or perhaps even complaining behind your back. So it is time to tackle the situation head-on using the logic and blunt speaking of the Swords to clear the air.

The negative aspect is the temptation to fight spite with spite – this is not the way of the Swords.

THE EIGHTS

The Eights are the cards of overcoming obstacles and restrictions, inherent under the rulership of Saturn, and abandoning what may be redundant. They are the cards of change and are full of movement, adapting and learning new skills.

The Eight of Pentacles

Often called the Apprentice Card, this shows a young craftsmen carving out Pentacles. It can appear, for example, when someone has been made redundant or a life path dries up and suggests that the best way forward is developing their skills in a different field.

The Eight of Pentacles says that you will discover a new practical or money-making skill; domestic or financial arrangements can change unexpectedly and you may move or refurbish the home; channel any restlessness into tangible improvements.

The negative aspect of the card is accumulating skills and not putting them to practical use.

The Eight of Cups

This is very much a card of Saturn and also the Moon in its full to waning aspect showing that one cycle is moving to an end. Waite's card shows a man leaving behind his eight cups and moving to a lonely mountain. It may be that he has ended some relationship, he feels that his spiritual and emotional paths are not leading where he hopes, and he has turned his back on everything that he has gained so far.

The Eight of Cups indicates you could be moving away from a redundant stage towards a new phase in a relationship that may be difficult or even accepting that some particular friendship or love affair has run its natural course. Occasionally it indicates a holiday with family or friends in a far-off place, perhaps after a setback.

The negative aspect is jealousy, possessiveness by others or any potentially destructive emotional attachment from which you can only be free by walking away.

The Eight of Wands

This is sometimes called the Up-and-flying Card because the wands are flying through the air. A card associated with travel and moving house, the Eight of Wands talks of a complete change or even a turnabout of ideas or beliefs that may involve physical uprooting, sudden enlightenment or a burst of enthusiasm. But since Saturn is involved you can be fairly certain that some obstacle or setback prompted the new approach.

The Eight of Wands may appear if you have reached a watershed where you need a very creative, inspired approach – perhaps a change of scene or a spring-clean in the attic of old attitudes. Spending a few days somewhere new can give you the breath of air you need, although you may go on to make a more permanent move.

Its only drawback is in leaving unfinished business behind you that may sour your return.

The Eight of Swords

This is definitely the child of Saturn. The Universal Waite pack shows a ring of swords and in the centre a woman who is blindfolded and tied up. She has apparently come from a castle we can see behind, so she has already made the decision to leave, but either circumstance or her own fears hold her captive. There is no one else around and she is the only one who can make the final break from what is imprisoning her. This is not a card of blind fate as is sometimes suggested, where she needs to wait for guidance, but one of struggling to be free.

If you get the Eight of Swords, you may be feeling very restricted by the demands of others or old guilts and responsibilities that you thought you had left behind. The Swords are the suit of logic so you must use your head, not your heart, to face down the fears only you can overcome.

The negative aspect of this card is waiting for a rescuer you do not need.

THE NINES

These cards are ruled by Mars and talk of action and the courage and determination to succeed whatever the odds, of self-reliance, of striving for perfection, self-confidence, a strong personal identity, independence or, at their most negative, total isolation. They are the cards of supreme effort.

The Nine of Pentacles

The Nine of Pentacles, known sometimes as the Wish Card is the card of security and independence, whether

in a material sense or a determination not to rely on others to solve crises. The card shows a well-dressed woman standing alone in the well-tended garden of a big house with her Pentacles growing and bearing fruit. It promises material success through one's own resources and efforts.

The Nine of Pentacles can signify that financial or material independence may be an issue, or perhaps you are expecting a major practical or financial change, whether a change of job, house or launching a venture that is important to you. Use the courage of Mars, for you have the ability to succeed.

The only problem with this card is if you do not really want the change or step to independence; listen to yourself for you may be happier as you are.

The Nine of Cups

The Nine of Cups is the card of self-confidence and emotional self-reliance, an ability to be happy in one's own company and sure of one's own worth. It depicts a man fenced in from the outside world by the Cups. His feelings are centred inwards rather than on others, but he is not unhappy.

The Nine of Cups may indicate that you are still searching for the right person or relationships may be temporarily less important than the fulfilment of a particular dream or ambition. Have the courage to follow your heart's desire for spiritual quests may override material concerns.

The negative aspect of this card is the emotional isolation of one who demands perfection in others and seeks ideal love, not a real person.

The Nine of Wands

In the Universal Waite pack this card is given the title of 'bloody but unbowed' as the young man who has appeared in many Wands cards stands with his head bandaged and presumably the staves of the vanquished behind him. He

has clearly paid a high price, and, as in all the Nine cards, the figure is alone.

If you get the Nine of Wands in a reading, you may feel as though you have had to fight long and hard for what you want, but success is assured if you keep your courage and determination.

The only drawback is if you really do not have the energy or impetus to carry on. If so, accept what you have achieved and do not push yourself beyond endurance.

The Nine of Swords

This card shows the woman so often portrayed in the Swords, covering her eyes to shut out danger. But the Swords are not pointing towards her and the enemy lurks within her mind. She may be haunted by memory or former failures and the old ghosts who have vanquished her and may need the steel and courage of Mars if she is to open her eyes to future possibilities.

The Nine of Swords is a card that reflects, rather than predicts, doubts and despair. As with similar Swords cards, the worst fears are within and can be magnified to the point where no solution seems possible. Only by breaking out of the isolation and seeking support will the darkness be dissipated.

The negative aspect is ignoring real current problems because of preoccupation with the past.

THE TENS

The Tens herald completion, which can represent either perfection or endings before new beginnings and new hope. As well as being the cards of fulfilment, they are ruled by Pluto, who eliminates all that is redundant in our lives. For life rarely stands still and often, as soon as we have arrived, we find ourselves *en route* to a new destination.

The Ten of Pentacles

The Ten of Pentacles shows the culmination of hard work and practical effort – the patriarch, family, castle and

garden – and speaks of following the conventional path and succeeding. It may also mirror the need to see ourselves as part of an interdependent unit and not separate.

If you get the Ten of Pentacles in a reading, you should achieve financial security and happiness within the home and family. Plans and practical matters may be completed or you may enter into a new permanent domestic commitment. You may find the ideal home or make the present one comfortable because at this stage the hearth is far more fulfilling than lonely shores or wild dreams.

The only drawback is if people become secondary to the financial and material setting.

The Ten of Cups

The Ten of Cups gives the same message on the emotional plane. Happiness lies through stable relationships, togetherness and family bliss rather than romantic love and passion.

I see the rainbow shown on the Universal Waite card as indicating that it is no good dreaming of perfect love and fulfilment. It is a card that occasionally turns up when one partner's thoughts are straying. We need to accept the reality of relationships as they are, with bad aspects as well as good.

If you get the Ten of Cups it may be that you have or intend to make a deep emotional commitment or have accepted that for now the family needs your attention. You have a lot to be happy about. The card may even appear when you are alone, but feel that it is time to settle down. Love and happiness are assured for the years ahead.

The only negative aspect is comparing other people's imagined happiness with your own – and finding yours lacking. Do not waste time regretting what might have been or will never be.

The Ten of Wands

The Ten of Wands talks of a heavy burden or worry that is soon to be lifted. The card portrays a youth staggering

along carrying his burden of staves. There is a great deal of confusion (as with the later Wands cards generally) about what this card says – even Waite is ambiguous.

But the Ten of Wands in a reading would seem to represent what has been achieved on the creative, professional or personal front. That is quite considerable, as symbolised by the Ten Wands, and there is success whether it be promotion or a realisation of a dream.

The negative aspect may mirror your feelings of frustration at being overburdened. It is a question now of off-loading any unnecessary responsibilities imposed by others.

The Ten of Swords

The Ten of Swords, 'the darkest hour is before the Dawn' card, continues from the Nine of Swords and has the morning breaking, promising a new and better tomorrow, the light at the end of the tunnel.

The figure is pierced by Ten Swords, but as nine becomes ten and a completion, a new beginning, there is reassurance of rebirth of the unique self.

When the Ten of Swords turns up, you may be trying desperately to fight a lost cause or hanging on to a dead relationship or stage in your life. It is time to accept that some aspect of your life is ending and it is a time to regret and allow yourself to be sad and rest before moving on. The sun will shine again for you.

The negative aspect is resisting the inevitability of change or in denying yourself the need to mourn. Cry what tears you must, then move on.

Chapter 4

Choosing a Spread

There is great mystique about spreads among some Tarot readers who claim that the more complex a reading the more profound it is. But really it is a question of finding the right format, depending on both the number and kind of cards you are using, whether a Major or Minor Arcana or full pack reading and the nature of the enquiry, be it a full life review, options between two or more courses, or a specific issue.

I have listed a selection of spreads that I have found helpful over a number of years, some of which were taught to me by experienced clairvoyants and some I have developed from two or three versions of the same layout. But the best spreads are those created by an individual Tarot reader for a specific purpose, rather than following positions other people have set down, unless these prove relevant to the question being asked. There are many forms of layouts, such as the Options Spread (see Chapter 10 on the Tarot and Numerology for my version), the Horseshoe Spread and even the Celtic Cross.

In addition there are layouts linked with the different sections, for example a Kabbalistic spread (see Chapter 9), a Calender, a Past, Present and Future format (see Chapter 5, Fortune Telling and the Tarot) and two zodiac layouts (see Chapter 6 on the Tarot and the Zodiac).

A Gestalt Three, Six and Nine-card Reading

This works with the Major and Minor Arcana and the complete pack.

The Gestalt school of psychology believes that everything is perceived in patterns and that the sum of the parts is different from and even greater than the whole. For this reason, a three, six or nine-card reading without assigning specific positional meanings to individual cards is the best form of layout, since the reader does not break down the reading into separate segments, but builds up a whole picture that *is* greater than the individual cards.

You can use a three-card spread when you are in a hurry or have a specific question to answer, a six-card spread for more detail or a more complex issue, and a full nine-card spread for a matter which is not so clear or may involve a major life change. This is how to proceed:

- Begin either with a question, an area of concern or let the cards unfold their message quite spontaneously.
- Shuffle the cards in any way that feels comfortable and deal face down three, six or nine cards in rows of three. Start from left to right for Row One nearest to you, for the three-card reading; adding Row Two right to left for a six-card reading; and Row Three, left to right, furthest away from you, for a full nine-card reading.
- Turn over your cards one at a time until all the cards are picture side uppermost.
- See whether you can get an overall impression before looking at the individual cards.
- Which card seems to hold the key to the reading? Ask this when you are reading for others and the questioner will usually tell you without hesitation what is the key for him or her.
- Begin with this key card and then either read the cards in the order you dealt them or again choose a card order that instinctively feels right. Again, in doing readings for others,

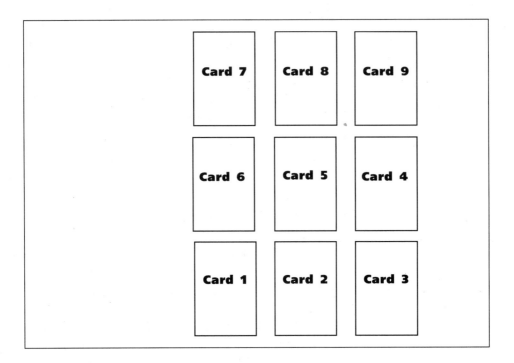

consult the questioner as to the correct order of reading for him or her. It is their reading and most people, given encouragement, will enter into a dialogue and apply meanings to cards even if the Tarot is totally unfamiliar – for these symbols are embedded deep in our unconscious mind.

- Note if any cards naturally fit together, for example the Emperor and Empress, and whether you immediately associate them or any Court cards with any individuals in your life. Ask the questioner for associations.

- If the reading still seems problematic, add more cards so that a three-card reading becomes six and, if you have dealt the full nine, add a tenth at the crown of the cards in the centre, as the integrating factor. It always works.

A NINE-CARD GESTALT READING
USING THE FULL PACK

Karen worked as a nurse in a busy casualty department, but her job was playing havoc with her home life, since she worked shifts including at least three overnights a week and one weekend in three. Carl her husband was pressing her to resign and had become increasingly remote, sometimes going out with his friends even on Karen's nights off duty. Karen loved her job but was afraid her marriage might break down.

Card 7: Two of Pentacles	Card 8: The Tower	Card 9: The Lovers
Card 6: Two of Swords	Card 5: Eight of Pentacles	Card 4: The Ace of Wands
Card 1: The Six of Cups	Card 2: Page of Swords	Card 3: The Devil

The Overview

Looking at the overall spread, the balance of Major to Minor cards was about the correct proportion so that the issue was both affected by inner and external factors. There are two Twos so clearly the reading is about choices and balancing priorities and this is echoed in the *Lovers*, another duality card. Of the suits, there were two *Pentacles* and two *Swords*, but only one *Cups*, suggesting that practical matters and maybe money, change and a certain amount of disruption took precedence over the heart – which seemed strange at this stage since the basic question appeared to ask about the marriage.

The Specific Cards

Karen felt that the key card was the *Six of Cups*, the first card, and then the *Two of Pentacles* which she said illustrated how she felt, constantly juggling her commitments. The rest of the cards she chose to read in the order in which they were dealt.

Key Card: Six of Cups   Karen felt that Carl was looking back with false nostalgia to the time he was a student and she a student nurse and time was much more fluid. Now she was a busy nursing sister and often had to stay late to complete the paperwork. But she said even in the early days of their relationship she was the one who made concessions and would go without sleep so that she could spend weekends with Carl.

Card 7: The Two of Pentacles Karen was, she said, constantly juggling her priorities so that she could take care of the house, work at the hospital and still be there for Carl, but she was permanently exhausted and stressed.

Card 2: The Page of Swords Karen identified this card with Carl whom she felt had always been immature, much as she loved him, expecting her to mother him while he went out with his friends. She said that it seemed he was using her work as an excuse to go out even more with his friends and that he had never complained before – until she had remarked about the amount he was spending on socialising.

Card 3: The Devil Karen said that she was feeling very angry, because since leaving college Carl had had a series of unsatisfactory part-time jobs in the art world and was now unemployed while waiting for his big break as an artist. If she did give up work, not only would he not be able to go out with his friends, but also they could not pay the mortgage. Indeed, she had to increase her hours because money was so short, although he said they could manage – hence the appearance of *Pentacles* and *Swords*.

Card 4: The Ace of Wands A new beginning in a creative venture, but for whom? Carl had been offered a job at a stained-glass factory, helping to design and make up windows to order, but he was reluctant to take it as he considered it was not proper art.

Card 5: The Eight of Pentacles Karen too had been offered new training, as a health visitor. That would mean that once she qualified her hours would be shorter and she would work mainly in the daytime, for a higher salary than her present one. But that depended on her taking an initial cut in money. She would not be able to do overtime while training as she would need to study as well as work, so Carl would need to take a full-time job.

Card 6: The Two of Swords But could she risk losing Carl if she insisted he took the job? She felt frozen into inaction and was closing her eyes to the situation, that Carl was drifting away not because of her neglect, but because of his own lack of commitment.

Card 8: The Tower Karen had so far avoided any confrontation. But she now felt that unless Carl made some practical effort in their marriage, she was coming to the point where the strain was too great upon her and the *Tower* of their life, restricted by Carl's lack of input, must inevitably come crashing down. Only if she stated her feelings might Carl see the reality of the situation and respond positively.

Card 9: The Lovers Karen believed that in spite of everything she and Carl could be happy together, but that could only be if she stopped making all the effort and let Carl have the choice of either taking responsibility or ending the relationship. A dreadful risk, but one Karen knew she had to take if the marriage was to be saved.

Carl did take the full-time job and Karen is starting her training. She knows that Carl finds it hard, but that he can only move beyond the *Page of Swords* if she stands back and does not accept total responsibility for his happiness. The absence of *Cups* in the reading no longer seems strange, since the need for change in their practical living arrangements and money problems were at the heart of the love issue.

Basic Spreads

A HORSESHOE SPREAD

This five-card layout can be carried out with the Major Arcana, Minor Arcana or the whole pack. It assigns significance to the position of the cards and this can be of special help in more specific questions or issues. The spread varies according to different practitioners so if the assigned positions do not feel right, experiment until the format works for you.

First, deal five cards in a horseshoe formation.

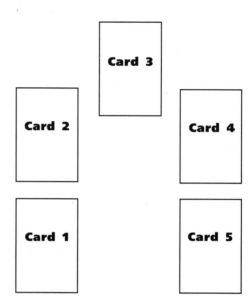

Read the cards from the bottom left upwards and down the other side of the horseshoe to the bottom right, progressing from the present situation or problem at the beginning of the reading to the final card, indicating possible advantage as a result of a decision to initiate change or to wait.

You may decide to formulate a specific question or let your mind go blank and allow the first card dealt to provide the real question. Unlike a three, six or nine-card spread, the horseshoe spread does not have a key card, but relies on the position meanings to build up a picture.

The Cards

Card 1: The Issue   Your present position and either the choice, dilemma or predominant question about some aspect of your life.

Card 2: Present Influences   These are all the people and circumstances that have contributed to your present position and who would be affected by any decision or change you make.

Card 3: Unexpected Influences These are partly the hidden factors that influence us, past successes and all the messages we carry from parents, past lovers, etc. They also include those factors we can just see beyond the horizon that will come into play according to whether we decide to change or preserve the status quo.

Card 4: Suggested Action Or this may be a conscious decision to wait; either course will alter the path that we would have followed if we had let events or other people dictate the future.

Card 5: Possible Outcome This suggests the potential consequences of our intervention.

THE MYSTICAL SEVEN SPREAD

This can be performed with the Major Arcana or the full pack.

Seven is considered a mystical and sacred number, symbol of spirituality and magic. The circle is the most magical of shapes, used in formal rituals as a protective area on which to work and also a concentrated place of power (see Chapter 11 on the Tarot and Magic).

- Shuffle the cards and arrange the pack face down clockwise in an overlapping circle of cards.
- Select seven cards still face down, either at random or using a pendulum.
- Place six of the cards still face down to form an inner circle, beginning at the twelve o'clock position and one face down in the centre of the inner circle.
- Turn over the circle of six cards, beginning with the one you dealt first, before beginning the reading, but leave the seventh face down.
- Read the first six cards in order as you would a story, seeing how the cards fit together.
- Finally turn over the card in the centre to reveal what is just over the horizon.

A COURT CARD READING

This can be carried out with four cards and is good for personal assessment.

- Shuffle the sixteen Court cards only and place them face down in a circle, dealt clockwise.
- Select four cards, place them in a pile and shuffle them.
- Dealing from the top, place a card face down nearest to you. Read this and then place the second card directly above the first, reading this before selecting the third, until you have the four cards in a vertical pathway.

Card 4   Who you become.
Card 3   Who will oppose you.
Card 2   Who will help you.
Card 1   Who you are now.

EARTH, AIR, FIRE AND WATER

This can be performed with the Minor Arcana, Aces to tens only in the four suits.

If you can discover in advance the strength that will be most helpful in a particular situation, you can maximise your opportunities and minimise potential conflict. The simplest way of finding your most useful element at a given time is to focus on a forthcoming event or issue and use your Minor Arcana cards, excluding the Court cards.

Your unconscious wisdom has an overall picture and is aware of factors that have not yet emerged into your conscious field of vision and awareness.

Each suit carries also an inbuilt strategy – as follows:

ACE of PENTACLES

Pentacles or Discs (*Earth*)   Find a practical solution, approach an issue slowly and cautiously, trusting the evidence of your ears, eyes and common sense, rather than the words of others.

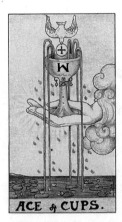

ACE of CUPS.

Cups or Chalices (*Water*) Use your natural empathy with others to see what they mean and feel. If in doubt listen to your heart and your gut feelings. Be prepared to go with the flow and co-operate with others.

Wands or Staves (*Fire*) Rely on intuition and inspiration. Seek a new or unusual approach to an existing problem or challenge and be prepared to explain and sell your ideas.

Swords (*Air*) Believe in yourself and use your head, not your heart. Be prepared for opposition, but if you are logical and ignore critics, not least the old voices in your head, you will succeed.

- Select the Aces to tens in all four suits, forty cards in all.
- Shuffle the cards.
- Cut the cards several times and begin to deal.
- Your aim is to see which of the four suits is completed first.
- You must begin with an Ace and cannot begin to lay out a new suit until you have its Ace.
- Keep to strict card order, with the Aces nearest to you, and each suit rising vertically from Ace to ten so that the ten will be at the top.
- You can build up a number row in the suit of the Ace/Aces dealt before all four Aces are turned if that is the way the cards fall.
- If a card cannot be placed in one of the four rows, place it face down on a new pile.
- If you have not completed one of the rows before you run out of cards, shuffle the reject pile and continue to deal.
- The first suit to be completed gives you the elemental strength which is currently needed in your life.
- If you are concerned about the chance factor, record your first results and repeat the process for as many times as you wish.
- If at the end of the ten or so deals, any of the suits are equal in number, use only these, reshuffle and deal to get

a single overall result. Remember to shuffle your cards in between each game.

More Complex Spreads

THE PYRAMID SPREAD

The Pyramid is a sacred shape, found as far apart as Egypt and South America. The greatest attention has been focused on the Great Pyramid of Cheops at Giza in Egypt, built around 2700 BC which seems to be the repository of inexplicable physical phenomena and also psychic and healing powers. It has been suggested that pyramids acted as transformers of cosmic energy.

The Pyramid Spread is therefore especially good for spiritual matters or major life changes. I used to work this in-depth spread with only the Major Arcana and the number cards, but have discovered that the Court cards enable different personalities and facets of personality to be incorporated, resulting in a richer reading.

It is dealt from a shuffled pack, from the right in four rows ending at the centre top. As it is a layout involving steps, it may be better to turn the cards over one at a time as you read them.

Card 1 The Question that is being posed either openly or consciously.
Card 2 The Essence, sometimes called the Root of the Matter, is the deeper, often unformed question or unconscious wish or fear.
Card 3 The Head or Logical Considerations. In divination and magic, careful analysis which stems from deduction and detecting a pattern, is a vital skill for the Tarot reader. Likewise in any reading what the conscious mind can learn from given facts is part of the equation.
Card 4 The Heart of the Matter. This is what the questioner feels and while the emotional response is not alone the best indicator of possible action, what someone knows

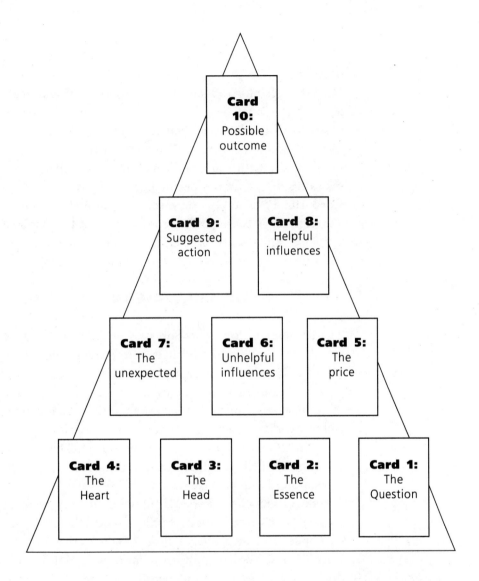

in their heart is right is too powerful an indicator to ignore.
Card 5 The Price. Any decision, however positive, involves loss and regret for the options not taken and the cost, not only monetary but also emotional, of any decision.
Card 6 Unhelpful influences. This can be any needless advice or criticism, however well intentioned, any obstacles that stand in the way of fulfilling a goal or even self-doubts. Swords frequently turn up in this position.

Card 7 The Unexpected. This is the card of seeing just over the next horizon to a factor that may affect your decision.

Card 8 Helpful Influences. These may be friends, colleagues or an unexpected source or even your own special strengths that will enable you to succeed.

Card 9 Suggested Action. A course that may alter or maintain the status quo, but which the questioner, rather than outside events, has decided.

Card 10 Possible Outcome, the Crown of the Reading. This card suggests the possible consequence of the proposed action. It is not a card of fixed fate, because circumstances and our responses to them are constantly changing.

THE CELTIC CROSS

The complex Celtic Cross Spread is regarded as a sign of an expert Tarot reader and it is worth trying for a very complex issue or an in-depth live review.

The Celtic Cross is not difficult to learn if you divide it into its three natural sections, then put them all together, and it works equally well with playing cards (see the *Complete Book of Divination*, Piatkus, 1998). This is also sometimes called the Gypsy Spread since it is very popular among Romany clairvoyants.

The Celtic Cross is best read with the full pack of seventy-eight cards. You can shuffle and deal the cards into three piles and pick one or deal straight from the pack. Place the cards down and turn them over, section by section and read each section before looking at the next. When you have read all the cards, put them together to determine a possible solution to the issue.

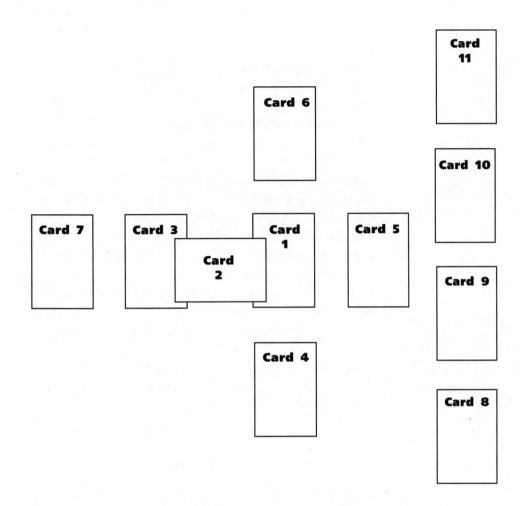

Section 1:
The Centre of the Reading

Card 1 represents the *Present Position*, the circumstances surrounding the issue or question, including past matters that have led to the current situation.

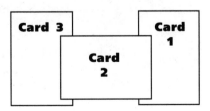

Card 2 represents the *Issue dominating your life* or the *Question you wish to ask.*

Card 3 represents *Obstacles to happiness or success.*

Section 2:
The Surrounding Square

These cards represent the underlying factors, based on the ancient elements.

Card 4, *Earth*, is the root of the matter, dealing with the practical considerations that may offer the key to a current problem or planned change.

Card 5, *Air*, is the logical factor that can separate what is possible from what is unrealistic and help to identify your strengths and potential.

Card 6 is the inspiration or *Fire* factor, the 'off the top of your head' insight that can make the missing connections in the equation. It can also reveal hidden dreams and needs.

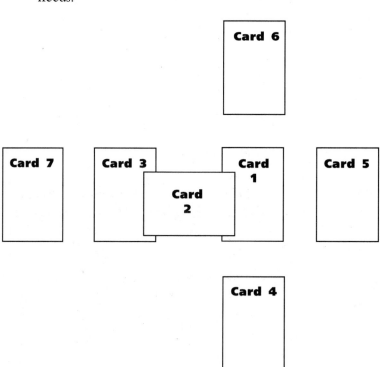

Card 7 is *Water*, the heart of the matter card, revealing what is going on under the surface, both in your own life and the worlds of those involved. It can also reveal your true feelings, which may be very different from what you consciously thought you felt.

Pathway Cards

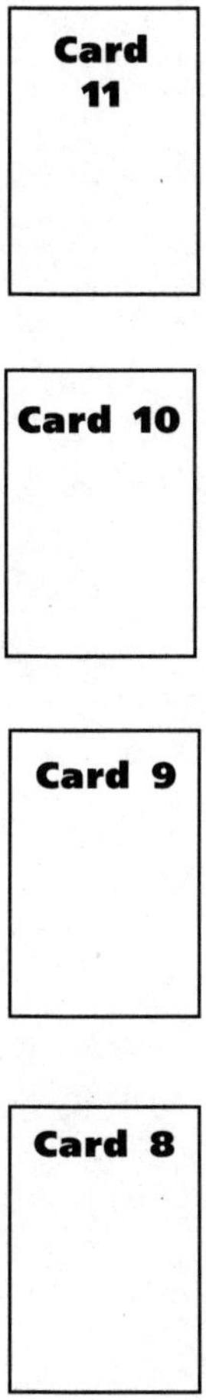

Card 8 *Suggested Action.* This involves a possible change or choice you may make.

Card 9 *Helpful Influences.* People or circumstances that can make the action or decision more likely to succeed. These influences may be unexpected.

Card 10 *Short-term Outcome.* This refers to the outcome of any change or action in Card 8.

Card 11 *Long-term Outcome.* This may be different from the short-term effects and needs to be considered in deciding if perhaps short-term sacrifice or possible disruption is worth while.

Card 11

Card 10

Card 9

Card 8

Part 2

Taking the Tarot Further

Chapter 5

Fortune Telling and the Tarot

Inevitably, when you begin reading for others, sooner rather than later you will be asked: 'What will the future bring?'

A clairvoyant or astrologer is judged by their ability to predict future events accurately. But telling fortunes is fraught with hazards, because whatever you say can influence someone's outlook on life. Even with the best of intentions you may unwittingly hinder someone's natural impetus to shape their own destiny by forecasting seemingly fixed outcomes. For example, someone who is told that the man or woman of their dreams is coming along or that in six months' time all their money and job worries will be over, may then decide that it is quite all right to sit back and do nothing while waiting for fate to deliver. But if the lottery win or wonderful lover fail to materialise then the questioner could be left high and dry with nothing to show for that time spent wishing and waiting.

Worse still, delivering bad news could shatter the recipient's confidence or sow distrust in a relationship. The questioner could then begin to behave in a negative way which could bring about the predicted disaster although it might have been avoided.

Yet time and time again I am faced with this dilemma when giving readings on radio or television. Someone who is ill or desperately unhappy begs me to tell them that better times are coming. All that can be done in such cases is to emphasise positive symbols and strengths inherent in the cards that show how the person concerned can move towards happier times if he or she does not lose hope and maximises their potential.

Can we Foretell the Future?

I have come across hundreds of cases where people seem to have had a vision of the future – in dreams, in sudden flashes of intuition and even in some cases in messages from the ghosts of their loved ones.

But at the same time I do not believe that our future is fixed. Rather, we face a series of crossroads and sometimes we get a glimpse of what might happen if we take one particular path.

A story which illustrates my view is that of Elise who lives in Dallas, Texas. She wrote:

'I called my mother very early one morning to warn her not to go to the sales with her friend later that day because something bad would happen. I'd dreamed I saw her friend's car wrecked very badly and my mother was in it. In the dream my mother was killed and I knew an accident would happen almost as soon as they set out.

'Mom asked me if I'd been drinking (I never touch alcohol). I cried and made her promise me she'd wait until the next day to go to the sales. She agreed but said she thought I was mad.

'That morning at 9.10, her friend went on alone. A truck jumped a red light three blocks away from Mom's house and hit the car on the passenger side where my mom would have been sitting.

'Mom phoned me to ask me how I'd known but I couldn't explain.'

It would seem that by her actions Elise managed to change the future. And this means that there is a point to fortune telling. How cruel and pointless it would be if we could look ahead and say only: 'Terrible trouble awaits you and there is nothing you can do.' Instead we need to be able to tell people how to avoid possible pitfalls.

Sometimes a flash of intuition will alert you that the questioner's current relationship will not turn out well or that their house move will be a disaster. But remember: it is not your place to pronounce definitively on such things. Instead you must help the questioner towards any solution which the cards indicate.

Tarot reading should be like any other counselling: a dialogue in which you interpret what the other person seems to be saying, in this case through the choice of cards – and it is for the other person to draw the conclusions about what path to take. A wise old clairvoyant once told me to never even hint at bad news. She said it was better to lose credibility yourself than to worry or frighten someone.

The Tarot Web

I believe that the Tarot can help us to identify potential change points before they occur, so that we can decide whether to continue on our present course of action or initiate changes. What these markers indicate is the combination of circumstances beyond our control with the possible choices we can make in reaction to those events so that ultimately we decide our own fate. Some spreads in this book do have a card of the unexpected and the Tarot is very good at providing glimpses of what is just beyond our physical horizon, although not beyond the radar of our intuitive senses.

Such wisdom is timeless and beyond reason, logic and expertise. It is that of the 'divus' or god within, sometimes described as the Higher or Evolved Self inside us all, the Wise One within who is not bound by linear time.

Perhaps the mechanics of Tarot predictions can be best explained by the concept of the Vikings' Web of Fate which they believed was woven by the three Fates or Norns, who oversaw even the fortunes of the gods.

The first Norn, Urdhr, speaks of the past which influences not only our present and future, but that of our descendants. The second Norn, Verhandi, tells of present deeds and influences which are also strongly implicated in our future.

Skuld, the third Norn, talks of what will come to pass, given the intricate web of past and present actions. Our fate or *orlag* is constantly being changed. Each new day the web is torn apart and rewoven in ever more intricate patterns and tomorrow's future becomes present and ultimately past.

The very act of discovering these change points allows us to anticipate and change our destiny.

THE WEB OF NORNS – THE INTERRELATION OF PAST, PRESENT AND FUTURE

This twenty-eight card spread recognises the concept that life is a web of constantly changing experiences and by laying out cards to represent past, present and future, the connections become clear.

- Use the full pack. If you have more than one pack, you can use two. If the same cards turn up in separate positions you will know they are significant, perhaps a stable factor in your life.
- Only use this spread once for yourself and once for other people, taking time to sit with the cards and study each one in detail.
- Shuffle and deal the cards face down.
- Lay out twenty-seven cards in three rows and then begin turning over the rows, from left to right, interpreting each card before moving on to the next.
- Read each row from left to right letting the cards unfold like steps on a journey.

When you have read the row of the future, deal a final card face down from the pack and turn it over. This card represents the Key to Happiness. Once you have read it the rest will fall into place.

The Key to Happiness card can be added to any other spread if the reading seems incomplete, once all the existing cards in the spread have been read.

Row 1: The Past
Cards 1–3   The gifts from the past that you should hold
Cards 4–6   Burdens you need to shed
Cards 7–9   What is naturally moving out of your life

Row 2: The Present
Cards 10–12   Helpful factors and people in your life
Cards 13–15   Avenues that may not be fruitful
Cards 16–18   Opportunities to be seized

Row 3: The Future
Cards 19–21   What is moving into your life
Cards 13–15   The short-term situation a few months along the road
Cards 25–27   Long-term potential
Card 28   The Key to Happiness

The Tarot and Time

The Tarot can be used for planning ahead by marking regular points in time. We can also home in on specific days that may be of significance, such as a job interview or a meeting with prospective in-laws, so that we can be prepared to maximise the opportunity and minimise potential conflict.

Finally, by looking at the links between past, present and future, it can be possible to shed perhaps unacknowledged feelings and burdens that may be adversely affecting our potential for happiness.

THE TAROT AND
SPECIAL EVENTS

Using the Tarot when planning a special event is helpful in two ways. You can find out, first of all, the predominant agenda of the other people involved and secondly the unexpected aspect that if handled with confidence can ensure the event is a success. By comparing two or three days for an event, if you have a choice, you can see which is the most auspicious.

- First write down the date of the day which is important to you in numerical format, i.e. 09 12 for the ninth of December.
- Shuffle the pack and select the cards of the relevant numbers (in this case the ninth and twelfth). These give you the predominant agenda and the unexpected factor.
- To find the possible outcome if you react positively, add together day, month and year and reduce to a single number, e.g. 09 12 2001 (9 + 1 + 2 + 2 + 1) = 15 = 1 + 5 = 6.
- So you would pick the sixth card face down of the reshuffled pack.
- If you have several choices of date try them all and see which gives the best outcome.

A SIX WEEKS AHEAD SPREAD

If you have a particularly momentous few weeks ahead or need to make a number of decisions, use the Tarot to tune into these key points.

- Six is a good number but you can add or subtract weeks.
- Use the full pack or if you prefer the Major Arcana cards, the Court cards, Pages, Knights, Queens and Kings and the four Aces, forty-two cards in all. Deal the cards face down and turn them one at a time, reading one then turning the next. You will choose nine cards in all, if you are considering six weeks.

Card 1
Where I
am

Card 2 Week 1	**Card 3** Week 2	**Card 4** Week 3	**Card 5** Week 4	**Card 6** Week 5	**Card 7** Week 6

Card 8
Where I
would
like to
be

Card 9
The key
to the
long-
term
future

THE CALENDAR SPREAD

This involves making a circle of twenty-four cards, plot-
ting the salient features for the year ahead. Use the full
pack of seventy-eight cards. In my book *Tarot* (Piatkus,
1999) I used twelve cards, but have also found that using
two cards for each month enables you to balance out
the positive and negative aspects. This can be done at any
time during the year but you might like to do it on New
Year's Eve during the last hour of the Old Year. The first
card for each month will give you **helpful factors** or

positive trends and the second **challenges to be overcome**.

- Shuffle the cards and, with cards face down, begin your calendar circle with two cards anywhere from the pack without looking, for the present or coming month in the 12 o'clock position.
- Lay down in turn twenty-two more cards in sets of two, set on each of the hour positions on an imaginary clock face, again selected at random from the pack for the year ahead.
- Turn the cards over one at a time, beginning with the new month or year, first the positive card and then the challenge of the month and you may see a month-by-month pattern emerging.
- Record the Calendar Spread in your Tarot diary and make notes each month and see how far it links with the months ahead.
- Finally reshuffle what is left of the pack and take a twenty-fifth card for the focus of the whole year.

Chapter 6

The Tarot and the Zodiac

As above so below, that is the golden rule of astrology formulated by the ancients as they watched the stars rotate round the earth through the year. The rising of certain stars seemed to regulate the seasons. As the stars seemed to rule earthly events, they assigned characteristics to people born when the Sun was in a certain part of the heavens.

But these astrological signs do give quite a strong insight into someone's character. When we combine the astrological symbolism with the Tarot, we have a very powerful divination tool. And there are many correspondences between Tarot and astrology. According to the Golden Dawn system, each sign and its ruling planet has a corresponding Tarot card and colour.

Two Tarot cards will have an astrological association for you according to your birth date: one for your Sun sign and one for the sign's ruling planet. These astrological associations are of great significance in general readings and I have listed suggested meanings that incorporate the two systems.

Astrology in the Tarot is not the same as pure astrology, because inevitably the joining of two divinatory forms changes their nature. You need no basic astrological knowledge to use the Tarot in this way, but if you are an expert astrologer, you can immediately move beyond the simplification to create a far more complex system.

The Zodiac Wheel

A good starting point is the Zodiac Wheel. The early astrologers divided the heavens into twelve houses along the ecliptic (the path that the Sun appears to take through the skies during the Earth's year-long orbit). The houses were named after the constellations on that path to form the zodiac we know today. To create your own zodiac chart, draw a circle and divide it into twelve sections as shown in the diagram (each section must be large enough to take one of your Tarot cards).

Each of the houses has an astrological significance. You will notice that just as star signs can share attributes, partly because they may share the same element or qualities, so the houses have some corresponding overlap.

The First House:
Aries, 21 March to 20 April
This deals with the self, individuals and core personality. It talks of new beginnings, change and renewal.

The Second House:
Taurus, 21 April to 21 May
This deals with possessions, financial matters and material concerns and security of all kinds.

The Third House:
Gemini, 22 May to 21 June
The Third House talks of relationships with equals, whether brothers or sisters, neighbours and interaction with others. It also concerns travel and communication, learning, study and memory.

The Fourth House:
Cancer, 22 June to 22 July
The Fourth House revolves around the home and private world of the individual. It also talks of older people, especially relations and all the issues involved in ageing.

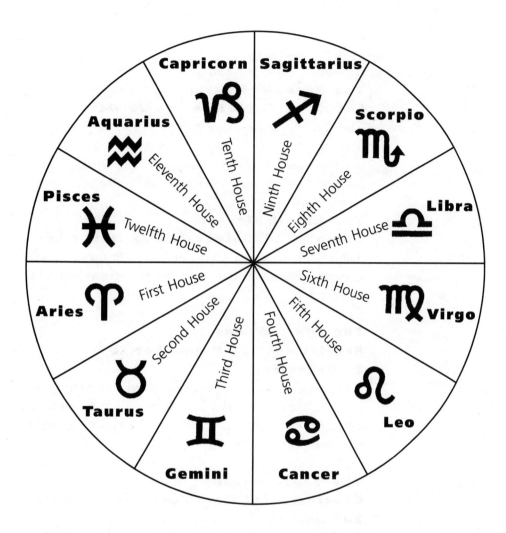

The Fifth House:
Leo, 23 July to 23 August

The Fifth House concerns love, emotions and passions. It talks of any emotional issues and strong feelings and is the house of children and younger relations.

The Sixth House:
Virgo, 24 August to 23 September

The Sixth House talks of health, physical matters and anything where detail is concerned. It also talks of work relationships, especially those you care for professionally or as subordinates.

The Seventh House:
Libra, 24 September to 23 October

The Seventh House concerns close relationships and partnerships, whether marriage or business. It deals with the negative as well as positive aspects and the actions of rivals and with any matter connected with justice.

The Eighth House:
Scorpio, 24 October to 22 November

The Eighth House concerns endings that form the seed of new beginnings, matters of inheritance, taxes and debts, psychic and mystical matters.

The Ninth House:
Sagittarius, 23 November to
21 December

The Ninth House is an extension of the Third House and influences philosophy and far-reaching ideas, distant travel, far-reaching communication, new educational fields, religion and new ideas.

The Tenth House:
Capricorn, 22 December to
20 January

The Tenth House concerns the outward public and social image as opposed to the Fourth House which deals with the inner private world of home. It talks of career matters and anything to do with officialdom.

The Eleventh House:
Aquarius, 21 January to 18 February

The Eleventh House concerns the influence of friends and organisations, and social activities. It also deals with hopes, principles and ideals.

The Twelfth House:
Pisces, 19 February to 20 March

The Twelfth House concerns limitations, conflicts, sorrows and difficulties. However, it is also the house of intuitive insights that can overcome any obstacles and lead to deeper happiness.

The Astrological Spread

- Shuffle the full pack of seventy-eight cards and divide it into twelve roughly equal piles. Then select one card from each pile without looking at the faces.
- Shuffle these twelve cards, then select one, again without looking at the faces, for each of the twelve houses, beginning with the First House and continuing anti-clockwise round the wheel. Each card shows the predominant trend at present in each of the areas of your life represented by the Houses and in the Tarot cards offers you select strategies for maximising opportunities and for overcoming obstacles.

Sun Signs and Tarot Readings

Cards in the Major Arcana correspond to an astrological sign. These are:

Aries	Emperor
Taurus	Hierophant
Gemini	Lovers
Cancer	Chariot
Leo	Strength
Virgo	Hermit
Libra	Justice
Scorpio	Death

Sagittarius	Temperance
Capricorn	Devil
Aquarius	Star
Pisces	Moon

There are other correspondences made in different systems so this cannot be a definitive guide.

USING THE SUN SIGN TAROT CARDS IN GENERAL READINGS

When your special Sun card appears in any reading or as your card of the day, it indicates that this issue is one of great personal significance and usually concerns your inner world or your reaction to outer events. If the spread has assigned positions, then the position in which your Sun card appears may hold the key to the reading. It can be helpful when doing readings for others to ask their Sun sign so that you can use this additional information.

If in a general reading using the whole pack, one of the Sun sign cards seems not to make sense, look at the astrological meaning whether or not it is your personal birth sign card or that of the person for whom you are carrying out the reading. See whether the astrological strengths and qualities inherent in the card offer help in planning future action.

You can also use the Sun sign cards in a whole pack reading as an approximate indicator of the best timing for future action or when an outcome of action is likely to be felt.

If, for example, the Moon card appeared as a future outcome, you might reasonably assume that the result would be experienced in the next Pisces period, mid-February/mid-March, where if it was in the suggested action position, February to March might be a good time to initiate change or begin a new venture.

SUN SIGN CARD MEANINGS

Aries, the Ram (21 March to 20 April)
Key word: *Assertiveness*
Tarot card: **The Emperor**
Those born under Aries are innovative, enterprising, assertive, free spirits with a strong sense of identity, energetic but self-centred. Therefore the Emperor card in its astrological aspect doubles its power for both men and women, but adds the focus on self development and innovation.

If this is your card, you can take control of your own destiny, and forge your career and personal development in new directions, but need to avoid overriding the opinions and feelings of others in your single-mindedness.

Taurus, the Bull (21 April to 21 May)
Key word: *Persistence*
Tarot card: **The Hierophant**
Those born under Taurus are patient, reliable, practical, loyal, cautious, with established social values, concerned with material comfort and security for self and loved ones, but can be possessive and lack flexibility. Therefore the Hierophant in its astrological aspect emphasises the values of traditional wisdom and knowledge acquired by patient application rather than inspiration.

If this is your card, you should rely on facts and knowledge in crucial situations, being prepared to wait for what is worth while in the long term for you and those you love. However, you need to avoid becoming so involved in the effort that you forget the reasons for your hard work.

Gemini, the Heavenly Twins (22 May to 21 June)
Key word: *Communication*
Tarot card: **The Lovers**
Those born under Gemini are adaptable, intellectual, scientific/technologically adept, inquisitive, intelligent,

communicative and adaptable, but restless. Therefore the Lovers in its astrological aspect says that choices in love and family matters involve the head as well as the heart and adapting to changing needs and situations.

If this is your card, you do need to communicate your feelings to those you love, but need to avoid a tendency to inconsistency and restlessness that can prompt you to leave rather than working through relationship difficulties.

Cancer, the Crab (22 June to 22 July)
Key word: *Sensitivity*
Tarot card: **The Chariot**
Those born under Cancer are kind, home-loving and nurturing, especially towards children, creators of emotional security, but secretive and can become over-sensitive to potential criticism. Therefore the Chariot in its astrological aspect says that balance and reconciliation between different family members' needs and viewpoints, especially children, are necessary if there is to be happiness at home.

If this is your card, you need to handle with sensitivity and tact potential changes in your home life – especially additions to the family or members leaving home. Avoid getting hurt by not taking any negativity personally. Do not hide your true feelings.

Leo, the Lion (23 July to 23 August)
Key word: *Power*
Tarot card: **Strength**
Those born under Leo are courageous, generous, noble, proud and loyal, born leaders, but needing the approval of others and occasionally arrogant.

Therefore Strength in its astrological aspect says that your many hidden strengths and talents will enable you to overcome the obstacles in your path and give you the courage to fight any opposition to success and happiness, especially if a long-standing struggle has been draining your natural energy.

If this is your card, the time is coming for you to take the lead in a matter of principle although this may involve sacrificing popularity.

Virgo, the Maiden (24 August to 23 September)
Key word: *Perfection*
Tarot card: **The Hermit**
Those born under Virgo tend to be methodical, meticulous, skilful, perfectionists, modest and efficient, but they can be critical of self and others, and worry over details.

The Hermit in its astrological aspects says that you should not demand impossible standards of yourself morally and spiritually, and should allow yourself the time and space to develop your inner world of dreams to put your life into perspective.

If this is your card, you may need to step back and let others cope with life, even at the expense of their being less efficient than you.

Libra, the Scales (24 September to 23 October)
Key word: *Harmony*
Tarot card: **Justice**
Those born under Libra tend to be balanced and peace-loving, harmonious, diplomatic with a strong sense of justice, but can be unwilling to make decisions.

Justice in its astrological aspect says that you are able to see both sides of any question and so may find yourself acting as peacemaker, but it warns that you should not forget your own peace of mind in the disputes of others.

If this is your card, you should use your natural ability for diplomacy to resolve matters where you feel aggrieved, rather than letting an unresolved dilemma fester through indecision.

Scorpio, the Scorpion (24 October to 22 November)
Key word: *Intensity*
Tarot card: **Death**

Those born under Scorpio tend to be psychic, mystical, intense, purposeful and regenerative but can be vengeful and introverted.

Death in its astrological aspect is entirely positive and concentrates on the transformative aspects of any natural endings or changes in your life.

If this is your card, it promises that, given determination and insight into the reasons behind the need for change, there will be a new beginning in an area where there has been stagnation, especially in matters of the spirit.

Sagittarius, the Archer (23 November to 21 December)
Key word: *Focus*
Tarot card: **Temperance**

Those born under Sagittarius are visionaries, seekers after truth and meaning, flexible, open-minded, extroverted, optimistic but can be very outspoken and can lack staying power.

Temperance in its astrological aspect brings compromise and moderation to intensely felt needs and desires, so that energies can be focused on achieving a goal and not dissipated by intense emotions or quarrels.

If this is your card, you will be able to integrate all the disparate elements in your life and formulate a clear life plan and how it can be achieved.

Capricorn, the Goat (22 December to 20 January)
Key word: *Prudence*
Tarot card: **The Devil**

Those born under Capricorn are cautious, quietly resolute, persistent, conventional and ambitious, with great self-discipline, but can be mean and very inflexible.

The Devil in its astrological aspect says that by following convention and social norms rigidly you may be denying yourself happiness.

If this is your card, you should fight against your natural

pessimism and let your humour and true, warm loving nature shine through.

 Aquarius, the Water Carrier (21 January to 18 February)
Key word: *Idealism*
Tarot card: **The Star**
Those born under Aquarius are independent, idealistic, intellectual, inventive and humanitarian, but can be emotionally detached and somewhat eccentric.

The Star in its astrological aspect says that you may need to strike out alone to develop new ideas, for everyone may not understand or see the world as you do.

If this is your card, you should believe in yourself and your ideals, for this is a good time to influence the world around you for the better.

 Pisces, the Fish (19 February to 20 March)
Key word: *Intuition*
Tarot card: **The Moon**
Those born under Pisces are sensitive, sympathetic, imaginative, intuitive, impressionable and spiritual but can be inconsistent and careless.

The Moon card says that you should trust your intuition and feelings, responding with your heart but not being misled by appearances and empty promises.

If this is your card, you may find yourself torn in two ways by different demands and people. Watch what you say and be careful what you promise.

Tarot Cards and the Planets

There are twelve Planet cards, although there are only ten ruling planets for the Sun signs, Mercury controlling Gemini and Virgo, and Venus controlling Taurus and Libra.

Like the Sun sign cards, the Planet cards can provide additional information when they are selected in a general reading. They refer to the effect the world has on us, whether in personal relationships or work or social situations, and indicate possible strategies to deal with things.

They are not related to the actual positions of the planets in the sky, but like the Sun card signs are an inner form of astrology, reflecting the symbolic influences and the psychic resonances with the different planets. The different Planet cards we select in our readings by some form of telekinesis (the ability to influence inanimate objects by thought) or mind power are those that do answer the questions we most need to ask.

Here is a list of planets and their associated Tarot cards.

Sun	Sun
Moon	High Priestess
Mercury	Magician
Venus	Empress
Mars	The Tower
Jupiter	Wheel of Fortune
Saturn	World
Uranus	Fool
Neptune	Hanged Man
Pluto	Judgement

The Sun rules **Leo**
Tarot card: **The Sun**
Sun deities are mostly male so the Sun Planet card focuses mainly on yang, animus or male energies in both men and women. The Sun is associated with power, creativity, vision, health and the life force, but also arrogance. In the Astrological Wheel method, the activities of any House that the Sun card occupies will be intensified.

The Sun card in its astrological aspect says that you should be confident and believe in your own abilities whatever others say. This double Sun power is the most positive of all — so make the most of any unexpected offers.

The Moon rules Cancer
Tarot card: **High Priestess**

The Moon influences the tides. There is also a hypothesis that it affects the flow of energies in women and to a lesser degree men.

The classical goddess Diana (sister of the Sun God, Apollo) was worshipped as the Moon in all her aspects.

The Moon is concerned with instincts, dreams, imagination, the cycles of life especially fertility, but also with illusion and is associated with yin, animal or female energies in men and women.

The High Priestess card in its astrological aspect talks about the importance of rising above any potential conflict or pettiness and listening to your inner voice, accepting that everything has the right time to happen if one waits – above all keeping your counsel.

Mercury rules Gemini and Virgo
Tarot card: **Magician**

Mercury was the Roman winged messenger of the gods (known as Hermes to the Greeks) and was the son of Jupiter. The planet is associated with the mind, science, technological abilities, logic, communication and with healing, but also with sharp practice especially relating to money matters.

The Magician card in its astrological aspect warns of less than honourable dealings by others and advises adapting your plans rather than confronting opponents, and listening closely to or reading carefully any communication.

Venus rules Taurus and Libra
Tarot card: **Empress**

Venus is sometimes known as the Morning or Evening Star, because she shines with brilliant silvery hue. At her brightest she is the brightest object in the sky besides the Sun and Moon. She is also the nearest planet to Earth and the closest in size.

Venus, whose Greek name was Aphrodite (born of the

foam), was beauty incarnate, the Roman goddess of love and seduction. Her most famous offspring was Cupid (or Eros as the Greeks called him), son of Mars or some versions say Mercury, so uniting love and war.

Venus is associated with love, beauty, the arts, all relationships, friendship, but also with excesses of love and romance.

The Empress card in its astrological aspect says that you should respond with your heart and not your head. But you must above all else love and value yourself, for unless you are happy you cannot fulfil the needs of others.

Mars rules **Aries**
Tarot card: **The Tower**

Mars is the planet with a reddish tinge. Red being seen as a warlike colour it ended up with the name of the Roman god of war.

Mars, son of Jupiter, was the father of Romulus and Remus who founded Rome and as god of both agriculture and war, very much represented the ideal Roman first as farmer and then as conqueror.

Mars is associated with aggression, speed in action and competitiveness. To his quality of courage is added a nobility of spirit towards the oppressed when the warlike nature is directed against injustice and inertia.

The Tower in its astrological aspect is a catalyst for casting off the restrictions and unfair demands made by others and above all says that it is important to fight for the freedom to be yourself.

Jupiter rules **Sagittarius**
Tarot card: **Wheel of Fortune**

Jupiter, known as the Sky-father, was the supreme Roman god, ruler of the universe. Like his Greek counterpart Zeus, he controlled the thunderbolts, which were carried by his eagle, the king of the birds.

In the Astrological Wheel system, as in astrology generally, the House in which Jupiter is found presages a favourable outcome in the area of life represented by that particular House.

Jupiter is associated with compassion, wisdom and learning, expansiveness and increase, the bringer of joy, but also with extravagance and being autocratic.

The Wheel of Fortune in its astrological aspect talks of maximising any opportunities, made possible by a change in external circumstances and widening your horizons both physically and mentally to overcome any difficulties imposed by the lack of vision of others.

Saturn rules Capricorn
Tarot card: **The World**

In mythology, Saturnus, the Roman form of Cronus, God of Time, was deposed by his son Jupiter. Saturnus had devoured all his children except for Jupiter (Air), Neptune (Water) and Pluto (the Underworld), the three powers it is said that even time cannot destroy. Therefore Saturnus had to bow to the inevitable. The old order must give way to the new. Saturnus was sent to Italy where he taught the farmers agriculture and engineering and he established a golden age of peace and plenty.

Saturn is associated with limitation, slow progress and difficulties, and in the Astrological Wheel, as in astrology generally, limitations may be experienced in the areas represented by the House in which Saturn falls. As the shadow side of Jupiter Saturn is the reality factor, the constraints of fate, time and space, but also challenge into opportunity, as Saturn found in Italy after his dethronement.

The World card in its astrological aspect says that though circumstances may not be easy, it is possible to move forward, given tenacity and patience, to a better way of life than which was led before any setbacks.

Uranus rules Aquarius
Tarot card: **The Fool**

Uranus, the original Sky God, was the son and husband of Gaia, the Earth, in Greek mythology. He and Gaia in turn created the twelve Titans, one of whom was Cronus. However, Uranus shut his children in the Earth so that they might not overthrow him.

Cronus castrated his father with a sickle, which became, after his own dethronement, the tool with which he taught the farmers to cultivate the land. Change can be cruel, but is necessary for progress; and like the sickle, any instrument or action can be used for good or ill.

Uranus is associated with sudden changes, originality, inventiveness and inventions, especially concerning tele-communications and also with sexuality, but also with impulsiveness.

The Fool card in its astrological aspect says that change should be welcomed even if it is imposed by others and taken as an opportunity for taking a new direction or learning new skills. If others are holding you back, ignore their pessimism.

Neptune rules **Pisces**
Tarot card: **The Hanged Man**
After Saturn was dethroned, Jupiter gave his brother Neptune (Poseidon) the sea as his dominion. Neptune's symbol of power was the trident or three-pronged spear (as depicted in his symbol) which he used to shatter rocks, summon up or banish storms and raise or sink whole countries. Neptune was unpredictable, sometimes offering safe passage to ships and filling fishing nets with fish, at other times hurling waves heavenwards in defiance of Jupiter and eroding the shores.

Neptune is associated with all emotions, sensitivity, with intuition, hidden potential and the unknown and mysterious and mystic, but also with indecisiveness.

The Hanged Man in its astrological aspect says you may have to give up security and the comfort of pro-jecting your emotions on to others and acknowledge your true feelings, negative as well as positive.

Pluto rules **Scorpio**
Tarot card: **Judgement**
Pluto (Dis or Hades to the Greeks) became the God of the Underworld after Saturn's overthrow. He took Proserpina, Goddess of Spring, into the Underworld and so brought winter into the world as her mother, Ceres, the Corn Goddess, grieved. He agreed to let Proserpina return to the world for six months of the year. But for the other six months she returned to the Underworld while her grieving mother brought winter to the world.

Pluto is associated with endings; with removing what is redundant to herald a new beginning; with hidden and unconscious powers, especially psychic abilities, with the ability to start again even in difficult circumstances and with financial astuteness and business acumen – but occasionally with a seedy lifestyle.

Judgement in its astrological aspect emphasises the need to wipe the slate clean and to leave behind resentments and regrets about the behaviour of others, however justifiable.

The Astrological Wheel of Fortune

This system is one that combines predictive and interactive qualities of the Tarot and basic astrology by maintaining the element of unconscious selection. The key of this inner astrology is that symbolic rather than predetermined connections are made with the powers inherent in the Sun signs and planets.

Below I have listed a summary of the correspondences, including colours, so that you can combine the Houses, Sun signs and planets in relation to the Major Arcana cards. You can, if you wish, colour the segments of your Tarot Wheel in the suggested rainbow shades.

House	Area	Colour	Sign and Card	Ruling planet and Card
First House	The Unique Self	*Red*	**Aries:** Emperor	**Mars:** Tower
Second House	Financial matters	*Red/Orange*	**Taurus:** Hierophant	**Venus:** Empress
Third House	Communication	*Orange*	**Gemini:** Lovers	**Mercury:** Magician
Fourth House	Domestic matters	*Orange/Yellow*	**Cancer:** Chariot	**Moon:** High Priestess
Fifth House	Love and children	*Yellow*	**Leo:** Strength	**Sun:** Sun
Sixth House	Health, detailed matters of all kinds	*Yellow/Green*	**Virgo:** Hermit	**Mercury:** Magician
Seventh House	Partnerships	*Green*	**Libra:** Justice	**Venus:** Empress
Eighth House	Endings, psychic development	*Green/Blue*	**Scorpio:** Death	**Pluto:** Judgement
Ninth House	Travel, new ideas	*Blue*	**Sagittarius:** Temperance	**Jupiter:** Wheel of Fortune
Tenth House	Career, officialdom	*Blue/Purple*	**Capricorn:** Devil	**Saturn:** World
Eleventh House	Friendship, principles	*Purple*	**Aquarius:** Star	**Uranus:** Fool
Twelfth House	Conflicting interests, intuition	*Purple/Red*	**Pisces:** Moon	**Neptune:** Hanged Man

THE ASTROLOGICAL WHEEL OF FORTUNE SPREAD

You will need a round, clear quartz crystal (about the size of a small coin) or pure white stone that is thrown on to the zodiacal chart to indicate into which House the card should be placed.

- If more than one card falls in a single House, then that suggests that this area is dominant.
- If your Sun sign card appears in a reading in any position, then the issue concerns your identity and personal world.
- If the card of your Planetary Ruler appears in any position in the reading, the matter concerns those close to you, whether in your personal or work world.
- If your Sun sign card or its Planetary Ruling card appears in the House associated with your Sun sign, it is an indication that the issue involves a major life change or decision, even if the original question seemed relatively minor.
- If a card appears in the House to which it belongs, this is an indication of harmony and appropriate action or decision-making, whether actual or potential.
- Using the Major Arcana only, shuffle or mix the cards and take a card from the pack face down.
- Throw the crystal on to the Wheel to identify the correct House. If it is on the cusp, take both Houses as an indicator.
- Place the card in the appropriate House and repeat until you have four Houses marked with cards:

Card 1: Your Current Strengths
Card 2: Your Current Weaknesses
Card 3: The Area in your Life you Need to Develop
Card 4: The Card of Fate – where future success lies

Chapter 7

Crystals and the Tarot

The late Scott Cunningham described in his book *The Encyclopedia of Crystal, Gem and Metal Magic* how crystals and semi-precious stones might be used to create a Tarot set and, as he states, this is a very popular tradition among Wiccans (the practitioners of a neo-pagan religion).

You can create a Major Arcana from twenty-two different stones and keep them in a special bag. Instead of selecting a card, you can draw three or more stones from the bag to read separately or to set out in any of the spreads described in this book that are suitable for Major Arcana readings alone.

Why use crystals? Because their living energies and the healing and magical properties associated with them can add a new dimension to a reading and provide an answer that may offer guidance about a spiritual path or direction. Crystals tend to bring out the positive aspects of the cards and so are especially good for inspiring optimism.

They have been revered and used for magical and healing work as well as for divinatory purposes by the Chinese, Native Americans and the Ancient Egyptians. Plato (427–347 BC), the Greek philosopher, claimed that stars and planets converted decayed and decaying material into the most perfect gemstones which then came under the rule of those planets and stars, and so affected the spiritual path of humankind. Scientists may scorn this explanation but there is no denying the remarkable effect of these stones on many different people in so many different cultures.

Although the Crystal Tarot can be used entirely independently of the cards, some people carry out two consecutive readings if a question is complex or has far-reaching consequences: first, they use a conventional three or six-card Major Arcana reading, then a Crystal Tarot reading. It can be valuable when selecting your Major card of the day, also to select at random a Tarot crystal as this helps to set the card in a longer term context.

Creating your Crystal Tarot Pack

There is considerable variation in opinion as to which crystals best represent the different cards. I have suggested twenty-two that work for me, applying commonly accepted crystal meanings, based on traditional healing and magical usage. Cunningham uses other Crystal/Tarot links which you may like to try or you may prefer to make your own connections.

In this case, take twenty-two crystals of different kinds, either those with which you are familiar from your personal work or indeed any that attract you in a store that sells a variety of stones. Mail order is not so satisfactory for this purpose as you need to handle individual crystals, which can vary considerably even within the same kind. You will need a variety of colours and types so that you can distinguish them in readings.

- You will need a bag in a natural fabric in which to keep your Crystal Tarot. If you are using the last method, place all your crystals in the bag.
- Take a Major Arcana card from a shuffled pack of the twenty-two cards at random, study it and ask silently that you will pick the right stone to represent it.
- Then dip into the bag and touch the stones one by one.

Look at the selected Tarot card and repeat its name as a mantra.

- When you have picked the right crystal, place it on top of its card. Continue the process until you have selected your twenty-two crystals.

Note the associations in your journal. If you cannot recall the name of a crystal, describe its colour, texture and what feelings are evoked by holding it.

Whether you use the crystals I have suggested or select them from a bag to make the connections, spend some time getting to know your individual Crystal Tarot and for a while use your Crystal Tarot instead of cards to select your significant Tarot symbol for the day.

- Spend five minutes at night selecting crystals from the bag and holding each one in your power hand, the hand with which you write, while gazing at the associated Tarot card and letting impressions come. These may be very different from your original card impression as the two divinatory forms merge.
- Next gaze into each crystal by either the light of a candle or sunlight while holding its card in your receptive hand and you will receive further insights and perhaps even see images in the stones.

The Crystal Tarot

The Fool	Clear crystal quartz
The Magician	Carnelian
The High Priestess	Amethyst
The Empress	Jade
Emperor	Turquoise or dyed blue howzite
The Hierophant	Lapis lazuli

The Lovers	Rose quartz
The Chariot	Rutilated quartz
Strength	Malachite
The Hermit	Desert rose
The Wheel of Fortune	Cat's eye/tiger's eye
Justice	Banded agate
The Hanged Man	Bloodstone
Death	Apache's tear (Obsidian)
Temperance	Blue lace agate
The Devil	Red jasper
The Tower	Snakeskin/Leopardskin jasper
The Star	Citrine
The Moon	Moonstone
The Sun	Amber
Judgement	Hawk's eye/falcon's eye
The World	Aquamarine

The Fool Clear crystal quartz
Known as the crystal of truth and a source of pure undifferentiated energy, clear crystal quartz is the stone of potential and promise. It has been regarded in cultures as far apart as the Australian Aborigines, the Chinese and Native Americans, as a powerful transmitter of physical and psychic energies and a manifestation of the living creative spirit.

As such it represents the living essence of divinity within the Fool, as yet undeveloped, that prompts him or her to approach what experience says is danger as opportunity. In terms of spiritual development the crystal quartz is the soul that is yet untested, but which compensates with that certainty that life is inherently good.

In your reading, your crystal quartz tells you not to worry about security or certainty or seek to emulate those who may seem successful in the world's terms, but who are in reality weighed down with material concerns.

The Magician   Carnelian

Colours: Yellow, orange and red, occasionally brown

The name carnelian comes from the Latin for flesh. It was regarded as the stone of courage and self-confidence. In the Middle Ages, carnelian talismans were engraved with symbols of Classical heroes and heroines to protect a home against storms, lightning and fire.

Like the Magician card, carnelian amplifies creativity and initiative. A stone of passion, both sexual and a love of life, the carnelian embodies all the positive attributes of this card, rich with energy and vitality.

Thus in a reading the carnelian represents the fire of inspiration, the magical spark that will risk all – and win.

The High Priestess   Amethyst

Colours: From pale lilac and lavender to deep purple, translucent, transparent and semi-transparent

The amethyst is the crystal of the spirit, encouraging gentle detachment from the need for the approval of others and the confidence to follow a personal path towards what is of worth and meaning.

One of the best healing stones for both emotional and physical ills which have been aggravated by stress and anxiety and addictions of all kinds, the amethyst, like the High Priestess card, promotes self-esteem and freedom from external compulsions.

In a reading the amethyst says that being alone is not the same as being lonely and you do not need the approval of others to be happy. Keep your own counsel, offer healing to any who need it, but look within for the seed of future happiness.

The Empress   Jade

Colours: Many shades of green, opaque to translucent

It is said that jade was a gift from the ancient Chinese mother goddess to bring health, prosperity and long life to her children on Earth. The Chinese used jade bowls for food to energise it with the life force. Jade was also regarded in the Orient as a bringer of rain, when cast into water. Gardening falls under jade's auspices and so jade has continued to be linked with the fertility and abundance of Mother Earth, and with the nurturing of children because of its gentleness.

The jade aspect of the Empress is that of giving healing through fulfilling relationships, kindness and a willingness to accept others for what they are and love their faults as well as their virtues, so destroying the power of the Devil.

In a reading your jade crystal says that what you give willingly now will bear fruit in the future and as those whom you nurture blossom, so you will be enriched in your own soul growth.

The Emperor   Turquoise or dyed blue howzite

Colours: Opaque, light blue/blue-green

Known as a male stone of power in Central America because it could be worn only by warriors, turquoise is regarded as a Sky stone. It is seen as a manifestation of the Sky and father gods in their most noble aspects, so endowing you with sufficient confidence and natural authority not to need to criticise or coerce others.

Therefore it accentuates the positive aspects of the Emperor: since you have so many strengths, you will find that you are called to take the lead and perhaps represent those who do not have a voice.

In a reading, turquoise indicates that you should be prepared to take hard decisions in furthering an important cause and that your own ambitions will be fulfilled through your altruism.

The Hierophant   Lapis lazuli

Colours: Opaque rich medium to dark blue with flecks of iron pyrites (fool's gold)

This stone is often known as the 'Eye of Wisdom'. The Sumerians believed lapis lazuli contained the soul of their gods and goddesses and as such would endow them with magical powers.

Because of this association with the wisdom of higher powers, lapis lazuli provides a connection with the higher evolved self and with angelic or spirit guides, taking you on a path of spiritual discovery.

The Hierophant in lapis lazuli makes connections with the past, with history and mythology and teaches others to value tradition.

In a reading the Hierophant crystal advises you not to cast off convention for the sake of innovation, but to take what is good from your own past and accept the kernel of truth, while rejecting the trappings of accepted authority.

The Lovers   Rose quartz

Colours: Translucent to clear pink

The stone of Venus, rose quartz, is the stone of gentle love, of reconciliation and of all family and child-related matters. It is the stone that takes away pain, especially of sorrows or abuse left over from childhood, soothes the fears that keep us awake, and heals heartbreak.

Therefore rose quartz brings to the Lovers, promises not of passion but of enduring relationships, with people of all ages, that can ease the sense of human alienation.

In a reading it says let love flow in your life by giving friendship and approval to all you meet and it will return threefold to you, albeit from a different and unexpected source.

If we can value beyond the outer form both in ourselves and others, then we can all find love.

THE CHARIOT.

The Chariot Rutilated quartz
Colours: Clear quartz with metallic, golden rutile, copper, or blue/grey titanium fibres

Rutilated quartz, according to legend, was created when angels froze the water of the heavens. Guardian angels were said to dwell inside it, offering protection and wise counsel to users.

A stone of inner treasures, it reminds us of our undeveloped potential, stamina and physical and mental strength so that we can make changes without fearing we will lose what we have, for we carry it within.

In a reading the Chariot crystal says that though change may seem frightening, it is the way to uncover unexplored aspects of the self and so to multiply opportunities as the inner store is revealed by new challenges.

STRENGTH.

Strength Malachite
Colours: Green with black stripes

A purifier and energiser, malachite replaces negativity with positive energies and pain with warmth.

It is known as the traveller's stone, because malachite is said to bring strength and perseverance to journeys both physical and emotional. Found in the mines of King Solomon and worn as an amulet against the Evil Eye, this stone was carried by wandering gypsies and sold to bring strength, health and prosperity.

Because it attracts both love and money, the Strength stone promises that all will be well and all obstacles overcome if you draw strength from others and accept that seeking support at times of need is not weakness, but part of a mutual exchange.

In a reading the Strength crystal says you should let others see your hidden strengths, rather than hide them out of modesty and equally acknowledge any temporary stress or uncertainty you may be experiencing.

The Hermit Desert rose
Colours: Light brown, rough textured, opaque with glints

THE HERMIT.

The desert rose resembles the stone of a fruit, but with glints of silver, so it is regarded like the rutilated quartz of the Chariot as the hidden treasure within, but this time the still centre of self, not the impetus for movement. It calms racing thoughts, enabling the mind to sort out priorities and step off the treadmill of life.

Like the Hermit card, the desert rose represents inner worth, searching within ourselves for the answers, and like the shamans or magic men exploring the instincts and the shadow aspects, as well as the higher realms of the self, so that the small but unwavering light of truth reaches and illuminates any darkness within.

In a reading the Hermit crystal advises waiting, listening and allowing events to unfold gradually, rather than seeking to influence them. In reflection all that has happened and will happen will become clear and the path will emerge quite spontaneously before too long.

WHEEL of FORTUNE.

The Wheel of Fortune   Cat's eye

Colours: Translucent gold or green

This is quartz with asbestos or chrysoberyl (Asian form) and is often confused with the more common tiger's eye (which can be substituted for cat's eye in your Crystal Tarot). Chrysoberyl is usually clear green or green/brown.

All these stones have an opalescence that resembles the eye of a real cat. So they are said to be excellent for promoting keen physical and inner vision. Cat's eye is a symbol of abundance, both material and spiritual, of confidence, self-esteem and healing of all kinds, as well as the independence and mystery of the cat who was sacred in Ancient Egypt.

These stones suggest, like the Wheel of Fortune card, that even misfortune can be used as the catalyst for positive change. By using focused vision, not least that of the Third Eye, unexpected opportunity can, if seized with courage, bring rich rewards.

In a reading the Wheel of Fortune crystal says that whether fate brings reversal or advancement, you should follow in hope the new path which will ultimately offer many opportunities.

Justice   Banded agate
Colours: Opaque, red, orange, yellow, brown and black
Banded agates are the true agates in geological terms. In Roman times they were specially prized and Roman craftsmen produced beautiful agate cameos using the many different coloured layers.

Agates represent balance and stability, security, the ability to assess people and situations. Throughout the world they were worn or carried as amulets of protection.

Therefore the banded agate in the Justice card offers the balance to deal with any injustice calmly and without clouding the issue with desires for revenge. It may be better to assess realistically the chances of outstanding matters being redressed rather than pursuing justice at any price.

In a reading the Justice crystal says that in any matters concerning principles, old wrongs, the quarrels of those around you, the legal system or officialdom, you should not allow your strong feelings, however justifiable, to take over your life – peace of mind can sometimes be achieved by compromise, leaving you ready to fight another day if necessary.

The Hanged Man   Bloodstone
Colours: Opaque, mottled green and red
Bloodstone is a stone of courage that links the user with higher states of consciousness. According to legend, the red spots seen on this stone were formed from the blood of Christ as it fell on green jasper at the crucifixion. So bloodstone is traditionally used in icons and religious carvings. Therefore, it is seen as a stone of sacrifice for a greater good, of letting go of the ego and material advantages to reach a deeper or new awareness.

Like the card of the Hanged Man, Odin, Father God of the Vikings, the bloodstone says that no matter how expert we may be in our own field or how successful we are in the world's terms, there is something important we need to learn right now that will give a new meaning to life, although it may temporarily seem to take you further from your objective.

In a reading the Hanged Man says that you need to open yourself to new challenges where you may risk failure, loss of face or status, but which will ultimately open a better way of life for you.

Death   Apache's tear (Obsidian)

Colours: Black

Apache's tear is named after a legend from Arizona. A group of Apaches were ambushed and many were killed and the rest threw themselves over a cliff, rather than be taken. The women and maidens of the tribe wept at the base of the cliff for a whole moon cycle and their tears became embedded within obsidian crystals. Those who carry obsidian will never, it is said, know deep sorrow.

When you hold your obsidian to the light, you can see new hope and life glimmering inside it. This stone eases and releases physical and mental pain, loss, sadness and anger, to allow the user to move forward.

Like the Death card, Apache's tear does not herald future disaster but talks of the need to shed those parts of our belief system that no longer hold the answers, perhaps the innocence of earlier days, and accept that certain doors are not and never will be open to us.

In a reading, the Death crystal says that you should face any regrets and sense of loss so that you can move into the light of tomorrow, for the world is full of real opportunity once you acknowledge your limitations and abandon blind alleys of illusion.

Temperance   Blue lace agate

Colours: Pale blue, translucent

Blue lace agate calms strong emotions, creating a sense of peace and encouraging patience especially with children

TEMPERANCE.

and older people and in situations that cannot be changed.

Like all agates, it is a stone of balance. It is rooted in the earth and cools strong emotions, especially negative ones, restores a sense of perspective and softens harsh words.

Like the Temperance card, blue lace agate connects with higher dimensions and mediates in situations where there may be opposing people or viewpoints, so that we can dislike aspects of others and ourselves without rejecting the person, a concept explored in the Empress and the Lovers.

In a reading, the Temperance crystal says that it may be necessary to modify rigidly held attitudes and to seek the best in others, so that we may evoke positive responses even from our adversaries.

The Devil   Red jasper

THE DEVIL .

Colours: Opaque red/orange

From early times jasper has been used for official seals and, like jade, is associated with rain rituals. The Native American name for the stone was 'rain bringer'. But in red jasper, the energy for rain and life to flow are pent up and the survival powers are held in check causing irritability, stress reactions and a lack of energy in every aspect of life.

Like the Devil card, this stone holds real power and potential, once we own it rather than projecting it on to others and making them into demons with power over us. We are the sum of all parts of ourselves and by the Gestalt principle the whole is greater than the sum of those parts, if we can see ourselves as we are, both angel and demon combined.

In a reading the Devil crystal suggests that you should not demand impossibly high standards of yourself and total control over your emotions, especially if you are being treated badly or taken for granted by others. You have a right to feel angry or frustrated and should say so, rather than turning the negativity inwards or blaming yourself.

The Tower   Snakeskin/Leopardskin jasper
Colours: Mottled brown or grey
Snakeskin or leopardskin jasper is the stone of wild places, whether the spots of the leopard leaping through the jungle or the snake who sheds his skin in the spring. This is the crystal of following the call deep within to leave behind the fetters of convention.

Like the Tower card which heralds liberation rather than destruction, this crystal is a symbol of spring when the keen east winds bring change in their wake.

In a reading, the Tarot crystal may appear when you are feeling claustrophobic, but fear the cold winds of change. But only by allowing natural progression and disruption, can you avoid stagnation and fulfil what is waiting on your life path.

The Star   Citrine
Colours: Clear sparkling yellow
Like starlight, the shimmering citrine is a symbol of promise that we can follow our dreams if we look upwards and aim high. Citrine clears energy blockages in the body, bringing mental and emotional clarity and self-confidence, for following one's star is very different from wishing upon it and hoping that those dreams will come true by magic.

The Star card in the citrine links the inner and outer worlds. The ancient astronomers identified the destiny of humanity with the movements of the stars – and we all have our special star that vibrates and resonates with our inner self.

If you get the Star crystal in a reading, you have or will have an opportunity, but doubt your own abilities or others may laugh at your dreams. Focus on your sparkling crystal and listen to your own cosmic calling that reminds you of the path you saw as a child, but have forgotten with adult cares.

THE MOON.

The Moon   Moonstone
Colours: Translucent with white, fawn pink, yellow, occasionally blue sheen
Moonstone is believed to absorb the powers of the moon and is reputed to become deeper in colour, more translucent and more powerful for healing as the moon waxes.

Moonstone is another stone of travellers, especially by night or at sea where tides are ruled by the moon.

Like the Moon card, the moonstone talks about the natural cycles of life, and its ebbs and flows. It reminds us that there is a time to act, a time to wait, a time to speak and a time to be silent. We can respond to these times if we tune into our innate rhythms and those of the natural world.

If you get the Moon crystal in a reading, you should tune into what your body is saying about your natural energy rhythms and not force yourself, if you are feeling tired or stressed, to continue without rest the frantic pace of modern life. Even if only for a few days, go with the flow of your desires and innate needs.

THE SUN .

The Sun   Amber
Colours: Clear yellow, golden brown or orange
Amber, an organic gem composed of petrified tree resin, can be up to fifty million years old. According to Chinese tradition the power of many suns is contained in a single pieces of amber and so it is a stone of stored power and accumulated knowledge.

As with the Sun card, anything is possible in the immediate future, but amber also promises longer-term happiness and achievement.

In a reading your Sun crystal heralds health, happiness, love, prosperity now and in the future, and endows the rest of the reading with optimism.

Judgement   Hawk's or Falcon's eye
Colours: Translucent green, grey or blue, tiger's eye-like quartz

The hawk's or falcon's eye is the crystal of clear, focused vision. As the hawk is one of the birds in myth to fly closest to the sun, it is a crystal of fire, purging away accumulated negativity and bringing enlightenment as to the purpose of past difficulties in forming what you are and know.

Like the Judgement card, the hawk's eye is a crystal of awakening, of regeneration based on tolerance of the weaknesses of self and others, and, more importantly, vision into the causes of mistakes that were constantly repeated.

In a reading the Judgement crystal says that you can rise above the past, not dismissing it but assimilating it like all aspects of the self as a necessary part of the formation of understanding. And so you can be free of its thrall.

The World   Aquamarine

Colours: Clear light blue, blue-green to dark blue

Aquamarine, whose name means water of the sea in Latin, has traditionally been the stone of sailors and fishermen and so is an appropriate stone as you travel forth to new horizons. It offers safety on all journeys, especially by water, and so as the Tarot path ends – and begins again with the Fool – so the stone promises that you need not fear as you move on, for you carry with you the protection that comes from facing all the demons within and without.

For, to the World card, aquamarine brings the awareness that what you put into the world you gain in different ways and that as you travel on land and sea it is also within and part of you.

In a reading your World crystal says you should therefore accept any new challenges with confidence – for you now have wisdom, yet retain the joy and spontaneity of the Fool.

Reading your Crystal Tarot

Place your twenty-two stones in a bag and concentrate on an issue or question. Ask the question, state the issue out loud or write it down to clarify your thoughts.

- Put your power hand, the hand with which you write, in the bag and touch each of the crystals in turn without looking or trying to identify them and pull out the stone that feels right. This first crystal will clarify the purpose of the reading.
- Take as much time as you wish and the question may become more definite or even change.
- Place this crystal in front of you and, without trying to fathom its significance, ask to be shown in the next crystal the best course of action in resolving the matter.
- Once more take time touching the different crystals in the bag and select the second crystal by allowing it to choose you.
- Set the second crystal immediately to the right of the first and then, again without attempting to analyse the meaning, ask to be shown in the third crystal the outcome of any action or change in direction.
- Once you have selected the third crystal, set it to the right of the second crystal.
- Hold each of the three crystals in turn, letting them speak to your heart and psyche, so that not only words, but also pictures flow through your mind.
- You may find it helpful to write down these insights in your Tarot journal as later even deeper meanings may come to you in dreams or at times when you are out walking or doing some routine physical task.
- If you cannot get any impressions from the crystals, close your eyes and hold all three crystals cupped in your hands. Without effort let a story form in your mind and without trying to direct it consciously. This will answer all three stages of a reading.

Crystal Tarot readings tend to be very rich in symbolism. Rather than trying to break the reading down, let the images build up spontaneously and do not consciously try to make connections.

Alternatively, ask a question for the first crystal then

pick out of your bag up to five more crystals without assigning any positions to them.

- Arrange them as you would a six-card reading in two rows of three from left to right in each row, bottom to top, in the order in which they came out of the bag.
- After you have read the crystal of the question, consider the other five in any order that suggests itself and let them create a whole picture or a symbolic story that will guide your path.

Chapter 8

The Tarot and Psychic Development

The reason that so many different origins have been claimed for the Tarot is that its images are those common to many cultures and ages. Therefore it is a potent focus for accessing the wisdom of other dimensions, especially if you use a pack rich in colour and detail like the Universal Waite. If you have more than one pack, experiment with them as you may find that one steeped in knights and fair ladies, for example the Morgan-Greer, may be good for past life work, while another with more stylised cameos such as the Classic pack forms a more powerful focus for meditation.

You can also use the same set of cards for readings and for your psychic development work. In my experience, a divinatory pack is already tuned into your unique intuitive powers and so makes psychic exploration easier; equally, your readings are enriched by the added significance with which your psychic work endows the cards.

Meditation

Meditation is an excellent way to get to know your pack. Simply by concentrating on a single card and letting its images flow through your mind, you can often learn more than by reading any book. Begin by meditating on one of the cards you select each day as part of your ongoing work.

Alternatively, take twenty cards at random from the

pack without looking at their faces, shuffle them and lay them in a circle face down. Use either a crystal pendulum or your own intuition to guide you to the best card. Some experienced readers work with an unadorned Minor Arcana, but if you are new to the Tarot or meditation, a Minor Arcana illustrated in some detail provides an easier focus initially. If you have not carried out any structured psychic development work previously, meditation is an excellent way of letting go of the conscious thoughts and strictures that can block the flow of unconscious symbolism that opens the door to other dimensions and to the wisdom deep within the psyche.

Tarot meditation allows the world encapsulated in the image to enfold you quite gently. Meditation is frequently a multi-sensory experience: rather than being cut off from the world, you may find that distant sounds or faint fragrances are heightened and become part of the fabric within the world of the card. Colours become richer and in the rainbow world of the Tarot story you may find parts of your hidden self unfolding quite spontaneously.

That is the beauty of meditation: rather than wrestling through books to find the meaning of the Tarot, you relax and, instead of climbing the mountain, allow yourself to float to higher planes. In the modern world we find it so hard to allow experiences just to happen. That is why even meditation has become hemmed in with rules about the right and wrong ways to do it.

As with Tarot reading, if you learn meditation as a skill and worry about following pre-ordained steps, you are actually putting barriers in the way of a process that is as natural as breathing. Those moments lost in daydream or reverie, as we stare into the embers of an open fire, watch sunlight rippling on water or listen to the cascading of a fountain or waterfall, without conscious thought or awareness, are all natural meditative states. Every child can meditate – watch them apparently engrossed with a toy. But we tend to lose this ability as we grow older.

Some people find it hard to relax the different parts

of their body when asked to do so as a prelude to meditation or other altered states of consciousness. Try this
simple method instead.

- Sit in a chair, with both feet flat on the floor; if you wish,
  support your back with a pillow and have armrests on the
  chair for your elbows. If you are uncomfortable, it is hard
  to meditate.
- In the sitting position, you should have your arms resting
  comfortably in your lap with palms upwards. Some people
  prefer to sit cross-legged on the floor with their hands
  supporting their knees.
- The most important factor is not worrying about maintaining a body position that may feel unnatural.
- Begin either at your head or feet, tensing and relaxing
  each part in turn, or if you find it easier use the following visualisation exercise.
- Feel your feet on warm soft sand and bury them as
  deeply as you can, pushing downwards and then releasing your toes to rest once more on the soft, smooth, sunny
  shore.
- See yourself enclosed in a rainbow bubble. Push upwards
  with your arms as high as they will go, so that they press
  against but do not penetrate the shimmering upper mem-
  brane, then sink back.
- Push outwards now to touch the bubble on either side
  of you, so that again you feel the pliable indentation and
  return your hands gently to your sides.
- Finally, visualise a beautiful butterfly hovering over your
  head. Hold your neck and shoulders, your chest and finally
  your abdomen motionless as the butterfly lands on each
  of them in turn and relax each part as the butterfly flut-
  ters downwards and away (a more detailed version of this
  exercise appears in my book *Psychic Awareness*, Piatkus, 1999).
- Alternatively, stretch like a cat after sleep, extending your
  arms as high as you can above your head, while clench-
  ing your two hands together; let go and bring your hands
  gently to your sides in a wide arc, sighing slowly out loud

as you do so and letting any tension in your body or mind leave with the sound.

- All the while press your feet down firmly as if pushing through the floor. As you relax, ease the pressure.

YOUR TAROT FOCUS

You can meditate with absolutely any cards and obtain positive results. Even an apparently sorrowful card like the Ten of Swords has its positive aspect: focus on the breaking dawn with its promises of tomorrow. But to begin with, it might be wise to choose light, golden cards such as the Empress or the Sun with vibrant colours. Prop up the card where you can see it easily without straining your eyes or neck.

- Work in the evening or early morning when you are sleepy but not over-tired.
- If it is dark, light two or three pink or purple candles to stand behind the card and cast gentle beams of light upon it.
- Light a gentle oil or incense such as lavender, rose or sandalwood to lift you gently from the everyday world.
- Do not begin with a specific question or intention, but as your body slows down, let your mind gradually empty by visualising your thoughts as water pouring from a crystal jug into a stream and flowing away down a hillside, or stars in a brilliant sky disappearing one by one until there is inky blackness.

THE SUN .

BREATHING IN THE LIGHT

When you feel totally relaxed, focus on a single circle or sphere of golden light or rich colour within the chosen card, for example the Sun itself or the globe of the world on the Empress's sceptre or the stars in her crown. Concentrate on breathing, slowly and deeply.

- Breathe in through your nose, hold it for a count of three (count slowly one and two and three) and slowly exhale through your mouth.
- As you inhale, visualise the golden or coloured light from the card entering your body and dark light leaving.

ENTERING THE WORLD OF THE TAROT

Become your breathing, while remaining focused on the picture.

- Continue and with each in-breath gradually visualise the Tarot image drawing around you so that you are within the card, bathed in its colours.
- Do not consciously attempt to move beyond the scene; that stage will follow in later psychic development work.
- However, you may find you do spontaneously experience visions of the past or pass through a doorway within the card to other realms. If so, accept this as a sign that you have tuned rapidly into your innate psychic abilities.
- Let the card world continue to expand and fill your mind, so that all other sights, sounds and sensations merge, and the everyday world recedes even further.

CONNECTING WITH THE ARCHETYPES

Allow any words and pictures also to come and go without attempting to hold or analyse them.

Where Tarot meditation differs from other meditation techniques is that you may perceive either in your mind's vision or externally a clear image of one of the Tarot persona who at this particular point is of relevance to you. It may not be the person depicted in the card on which you are meditating and you may hear actual words in your head that are emanating from your own inner treasure store.

- When you are ready, gradually move away from the focus, connecting with your breathing once more and letting the colours fade. As you do this external sounds will return and your normal range of vision expands until you are fully aware again.
- Frequently the Tarot image will spontaneously begin to fade or the external world intrude and this is a sign that your meditation is complete. Meditation is not a marathon; the richest experiences can sometimes occur in a meditation of five minutes.
- Stretch your arms and legs again like a cat waking after a long sleep, slowly, luxuriating in your relaxed state.
- Spend the time before sleep sitting in the candlelight, letting the Tarot world flow in and out of your consciousness. In the stillness you may hear more words or see images in the candle flame. This time after meditation can be as rewarding as the experience itself.

Astral Projection

Out of body experiences are far more common than might be expected. More than a third of people in the Western world have reported the sensation of spontaneously flying or floating beyond the confines of the physical body whether momentarily or visiting familiar places and people who may be suddenly aware of the visitor's presence. This is known as etheric projection and is so close to true astral projection as to be virtually indistinguishable in quality or intensity.

True astral projection tends to be more akin to a visionary state experienced during dreams, daydreams or in meditation, involving other places and times or different dimensions. These otherworldly realms can, on occasions, seem almost like the sky and underworlds described by shamans or magic men and women throughout the world on their psychic journeyings. You may find lands peopled by fabulous creatures, talking animals and rich earth or seascapes, that symbolise human experience at its richest or heavenly realms where we may talk to deceased relatives, guardian angels, spirit guides or our own evolved Self.

The Tarot with its deep psychic roots is one of the best and easiest mediums to evoke this waking dream state, in which we are aware that we are experiencing such places through our psyche and so can control the experience in the same way that people control their dreams when lucid dreaming.

Far from being an occult or dangerous practice, these astral journeys do have a deep religious and spiritual significance and have inspired many great artists, writers and mystics. Moreover, these otherworldly wanderings are self-limiting; you find that as with meditation the conscious world intrudes or you fall asleep when the psyche is ready to return. However, as with all psychic work and Tarot readings, you should work only when you are feeling calm, and negative emotions are best expelled by physical activity like digging the garden or scrubbing the kitchen floor before beginning.

CROSSING THE THRESHOLD

Certain cards seem more potent than others and the Major Arcana in practice seems the most evocative for astral travel. However, certain cards from the Minor Arcana are also very effective:

- Eight of Wands, the up and flying card;
- Six of Swords in packs where the boatman is depicted carrying the passenger to calmer waters;
- Two or Three of Wands with a figure gazing towards an open vista;
- Ten of Cups whose rainbow offers a pathway across the sky.

The Major Arcana cards listed below are ones I have used successfully in this field. But do experiment with different cards until you find those in tune with your own psyche. You may settle on one or two cards that you use as a focus for your astral work, or work with a larger number and choose an astral card either by the pendulum method described in the Introduction to this book or by spreading the Major Arcana plus any of the Minor cards that feel right in a circle face downwards. Touch or hold each in turn, asking silently to be shown the right card for your work on this particular occasion.

For astral projection, I steer away from more complex cards such as Death, the Devil, the Tower and the Hanged Man. Although there is nothing inherently negative about them, you cannot roam freely through their portals without exploring the deeper implications of the shadow as well as positive aspects of these symbols. This is a process you may need to work on through meditation and divination for many months in order to have entirely positive astral experiences using these cards.

THE GATEWAY CARDS

The Fool: Follow the direction in which the Fool is leaping or stepping. Your flying or floating sensation will begin as you leave the cliff of certainty and restriction. In the Waite pack, the Fool is looking upwards so he will float or fly rather than fall.

The Magician: His wand will guide you on the right path which in the Universal Waite pack may be upwards. But you can also follow his finger downwards into a tunnel through the earth which may lead to the same place remembering his 'As above, so below'.

The High Priestess: Walk between two pillars and through the veil of the Sacred Temple. Study the wisdom on the scroll she holds for it contains answers to questions you did not know you needed to ask.

The Empress: Hers is the way of nature. Take the path beyond the waterfall, into the instinctual forest, or across the cornfields. On either route you may find friendly animals that help you on your way.

The Hierophant: Behind his throne is the doorway of

light into the spiritual dimension that is his domain. If your card shows the crossed keys at the Hierophant's feet, these will open any door. But remember to return them.

The Chariot: Ride behind the hero as he leaves the city in his chariot to journey through unknown lands, in his search for knowledge and understanding. His wanderings may take you to the future or the past.

The Hermit: He stands on the tops of the mountains looking down, for his is the inner journey. The landscape below may be shrouded in mist, but the Hermit's lamp will ensure you do not become lost as he leads you to his cave from where many shamanic journeys begin.

The Wheel of Fortune: The Egyptian/classical symbolism in the Waite pack may suggest that the ancient past and future are spokes of the same wheel. It is a card to choose at a time of imminent or potential change with the Sphinx *couchant* at the top of the Wheel, Anubis, the Egyptian jackal-headed god and protector of the dead supporting the Wheel and the Greek Typhon in his serpent form descending.

Temperance: Let Iris, Goddess of the Rainbow, show you angels, nature spirits and perhaps your own special spirit guide. Or if your pack depicts an angel, let her guide and protect you.

The Star: Perhaps the richest card for all astral travel. Gaze into the pool like the maiden as she pours the Waters of Life upon the earth – or, like the heroes of fairy tales, dive deep into the pool to an underwater realm where treasure lies. Or follow your own special star. Perhaps you might begin by flying on the wings of the bird, waiting on the tree.

The Moon: Follow the golden path of moonbeams as the Moon Mother draws up the discarded thoughts and memories of humankind every evening to be renewed and transformed into healing dew. Or, like the crayfish in many Moon cards, swim deep in the sea that goes back to the Dawn of Time and may carry you anywhere.

The Sun: Ride with the child on the white horse in

THE STAR.

the noonday sun or climb the sunflowers beyond the wall upwards on the pathway to the sun itself.

The World: Move within the cosmic egg of creation and rebirth with the dancer who gathers all that has gone before into a harmonious whole and, like the shamans, dance your way out of your body.

CROSSING THE GATEWAY OF LIGHT

- Light an incense of astral travel (frankincense, jasmine or sandalwood) and make a semi-circle of pure white candles or a large circular white lamp to stand behind your card or an enlarged card copy.
- Extinguish all other lights so that the rest of the room is in shadow.
- A good time to do this, although you may not wish to use candles or incense in this case, is that period of half-sleep very early just before dawn.
- As with meditation, you may want to relax your body, but in the early morning you may already be in this state.
- Breathe in gently and exhale as for meditation, with each inhaled breath drawing yourself upwards and into the card.
- Do not scorn the imagination which is the doorway to the psyche and if you visualise your etheric or spirit double rising, in time the process will become quite natural.
- Identify an opening within your card, a door or a window that appears as you move further into the card.
- You may find it easier to concentrate on one point in the stimulus, seeing it as a curtain which opens or a coloured circle which melts and admits you within.
- There may be mist through the door but go through and you will find yourself floating, flying or swimming effortlessly through water, or travelling down through tunnels into the earth.
- You may experience a slight sensation as you pass through the doorway of light or the curtain. If you cannot, again let your imagination guide you through.

- Waiting will be a guide, a Tarot character, perhaps one you met in meditation who this time will make him or herself known, who will lead you and care for you as you move through these magical realms and will take you back to the light when it is time to return.

- Often one of the Queens will assume this role, but you may find that the King of Pentacles has the patience and wisdom to direct you to what you need to see. If you are uncertain, a Page may guide you. If it is one of the Knights, he is more likely to gallop through the lands with you and let you gain your own impressions. Your guide may change for different journeys.

KING of PENTACLES

Past Life Exploration

Reincarnation, the belief that our soul returns to a new body after death, has been accepted by about two-thirds of the world's population, mainly in the East, for thousands of years. In the Western world also, with the growing interest in Eastern religions, the belief that we may have had many lives is finding support in the light of recent evidence, especially from young children who may recall details of former existences that are subsequently verified by independent research into the places and times named by the child.

Jung's belief in the universal tribal memory, called the Collective Unconscious or Great Memory, explains past life memories in terms of tapping into a particular archetypal symbol from the past with which our present situation or need is linked or synchronised. Either way, the Tarot is an ideal medium for contacting the past.

BEGINNING PAST LIFE TAROT WORK

In a sense the division between astral travel and past life work is quite artificial as you can travel spontaneously through your Tarot astral exploration to different ages, especially with the Gateway cards listed on pages 170–172.

If you specifically wish to explore the past, whether your own past lives or those of people who are linked spiritually with you, you can focus on moving backwards through time.

As well as the cards already listed for astral travel, the Four and Six of Cups are very effective. In the former an invisible hand offers ethereal cups to the figure seated by the tree, in the latter, a card associated in divination with looking to the past, there is an old town to be explored and the figures to follow. The Four of Wands and the Ten of Pentacles also offer towns that are rich in potential.

The four Aces also seem powerful for past life exploration because of their spiritual symbolism. In the Universal Waite Tarot and many others they are based on the Grail symbols (see Chapter 11 on the Tarot and Magic).

THE MIRROR AND CANDLE TECHNIQUE

The mirror and candle technique is one of the best methods to approach any past life work. Tarot past life journeys are remarkably simple, no trances, no long preparations, for the card holds all you will need to visit the past, using the archetypal symbols to transport you back to the worlds of their origins.

- Begin as near to midnight as you can.
- Burn an incense of past life work, like myrrh, mimosa or cedar.
- Take a large oval mirror and place three small white candles diagonally in a line so that they form a pathway to and within the mirror.
- Take all the cards that seem to you possibilities – you do not need only to use ones I have suggested – and one by one turn them over, discarding in one pile any that do not seem right on this occasion.

- It is worth enlarging on a photocopier or computer in advance, a core number of images: especially the Gateway cards and the Aces.

- Add to their number any that feel right for past life work, perhaps ones you selected over a period of days or in a number of readings, especially if you are currently working with issues from the past.

- Keep eliminating cards on each occasion you begin past life work until you are left with one which feels right. Study each card for as long as you wish as you narrow down your choices.

- Prop your chosen Tarot card with its back to you so that you can see the image reflected in the mirror close to the candle furthest from the mirror.

- Experiment with placing until your card looks like a doorway into a world, which it *is* symbolically.

- Memorise the card in detail before you extinguish the lights as you will no longer see it clearly with your physical eye.

- When you are ready, extinguish all lights except the candles and as you inhale the light and exhale darkness, project yourself along the path of candles.

- You may feel a slight resistance as you enter the card world.

- Continue and in your mind's eye see the Tarot image framed in a golden doorway of light that gets larger and larger.

- Enter the scene and you may again meet a guide, who this time will probably not be a Tarot character, but a figure you have seen in dreams or daydreams, someone wise and kind whom you feel you have known all your life.

- You may begin in the Tarot scene portrayed in the card, but will, with your guide, move to the next room or outdoors or enter a building.

- Spend time exploring this first world, although it is only a transition to the second world of the past time and place that is of most relevance to you at this point in time.

- Listen and learn. Other people will enter the scenes whose words will be of importance for you.

- When you are ready, look for a second door or entrance that leads not back through the mirror but beyond into a past life that could be a hundred or ten thousand years ago; again looking for someone who seems familiar. You are with your guide and this is only a symbolic journey so nothing can harm you. Here too you will enter buildings and see and hear people – perhaps one in particular with whom you feel strong identification.
- It is in this world that you will understand the purpose of your journey – watch and listen.
- Occasionally this may explain why you feel afraid of a particular aspect of your daily life or seem constantly to find yourself in an unrewarding situation or relationship.
- However, most journeys down the Tarot pathway to the past gently add to your own connections with and understanding of the past that holds so many keys to present and future. When you are ready go back through the door and spend a few moments in the Tarot card whose scene may have subtly changed.
- Look round and you will see the candle waiting to guide you back through the mirror, then through the first doorway of light into the darkness, illuminated by the candles.
- Thank your guide who may have final words of wisdom for you.
- Return through the mirror and follow the candles.
- Sit quietly for a few moments looking at the pathway you travelled and when you are ready blow out the candles one by one, sending light to any who may need it.
- Sleep with the chosen card under your pillow. Your dreams will be rich and will perhaps transport you back along your candle path to the Tarot world that was your stepping-off point and even to the second world where the *other you* took form.

Chapter 9

The Kabbalah and the Tarot

The Kabbalah is an ancient body of esoteric and magical wisdom from the Hebrew tradition that offers a profound personal path whereby the individual can explore the connections between humanity and the Ultimate Creative Source. Through its study and application through meditation and divination, the individual can move through stages of enlightenment to strive for spiritual unity with the supreme force behind the universe. The word 'Kabbalah' (also spelled Cabala or Qabalah) is derived from the Hebrew word meaning 'to receive' and symbolises the acceptance of wisdom. Central to this wisdom is the Tree of Life, a blueprint for the universe, an attempt to demonstrate the interconnectedness of all life and experience and a chart through life. The Tree of Life in its spheres and pathways shows how the pure undifferentiated source of light and life flows down into the material world. Each of its sephiroth or spheres represents one facet of experience. The lowest, Malkuth, the Kingdom, represents the material world. The highest, Kether, the Crown, is the source of quintessence. Between these are sephiroth representing other powers and qualities, intelligence, beauty, justice and harmony.

The Tree represents not only the process of creation, but also the workings of the human mind. Its paths run in two directions: the pathways from God to man and those which man must travel to reach the Godhead. This is the path travelled by the unborn soul as he or she is incarnated and travelled in reverse order in dying. However, by magic and divination it can be possible to connect with the higher realms during life.

Each sephira represents parts of the mind or soul. Using the knowledge of potential paths discovered through divination or meditation, a Kabbalistic seeker focuses on the appropriate strengths or qualities of the chosen spheres and adjoining paths to transfer strength from one part of his or her being to an area of weakness. Thereby he or she can change him or herself and sometimes influence the world.

It is said that Moses was given not only the Torah, the sacred written tradition by God, but also a secret oral law, which passed from generation to generation and it is this oral law that, it is believed, is associated with the Kabbalah.

Kabbalistic lore relates that the diagram of the Tree of Life was also handed down to Moses by God. The tradition was embraced eagerly by the alchemists who saw it as a way of uniting the lore of the great mystical traditions; those of the Egyptians, the Greeks, the Hebrews, the Babylonians and the early Christians. The two main books of the Kabbalah are the Sepher Yetzirah which was written some time between the second and sixth centuries AD and the Zohar, written in the thirteenth century by Moses de Leon.

Reading from the top of the Tree downwards the spheres are arranged in three triangles, with the tenth Malkuth separate at the bottom to form the four worlds. Each triangle contains two opposing forces and a third factor, the common centre which holds them together and transcends the separate spheres.

In the Kabbalah, the world is not created by a maker, but by a light or ray emanating or flowing from the Godhead which divides and becomes the sephiroth, the splendid lights or shining sapphires that are the aspects of the divine contained in all life forms.

The sephiroth are connected by twenty-two lines or paths, each of which takes the name of one of the letters of the Hebrew alphabet. Each path can also carry its association with one of the Major Arcana cards.

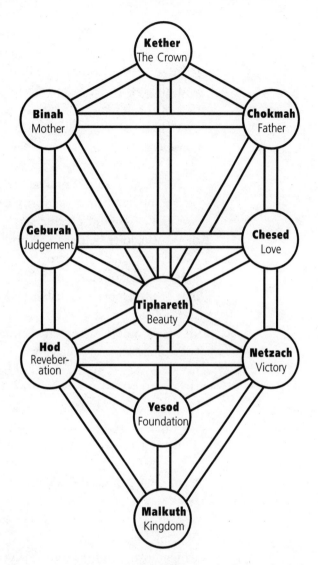

The Tarot and the Kabbalah

THE KABBALAH AND
THE MAJOR ARCANA

The first real connections between the Tarot and the Kabbalah were made around 1856 by Eliphas Levi (who has already been mentioned in the Introduction to this book). He noticed the correspondence between the twenty-two tarot trumps and the twenty-two letters of the Hebrew alphabet and became convinced as he studied the ancient lore, especially the Sepher Yetzirah, that with the loss of the Sovereign Priesthood and the destruction of the Temple in Israel, secret wisdom was concealed by Kabbalists in the symbolism of Tarot cards. Indeed, he considered that were one to have only a Tarot pack, it was still possible to acquire a great deal of knowledge.

Although it seems unlikely that the Tarot cards existed before medieval times, nevertheless the connection is one that makes sense in psychic and spiritual terms. In numerology also, long before the Tarot was created, the number twenty-two had come to encapsulate totality, the whole universe, wisdom and truth because of the number meanings of the Hebrew alphabet (see Chapter 10 on the Tarot and Numerology).

I have only scratched the surface of Kabbalistic knowledge since this is primarily a book on the Tarot and I have not talked in any detail either about the vertical pillars or the different realms. But the Tree of Life can form the basis of a powerful personal divination system that is not difficult to approach and yet can offer spiritual enlightenment, even with the most rudimentary knowledge.

THE KABBALAH AND THE MINOR ARCANA

The rest of the Tarot deck was also linked by Levi to the Tree of Life, each of the ten sephiroth having a number which correlates with one of the ten number cards in the Tarot suits. The four suits and kinds of Court card correspond to the Four Worlds of creation as represented on the Tree. But here I have concentrated on the all-important Tarot trumps.

The Pathways

The system I have used here draws heavily on the Western Mystery tradition, and especially that of the Golden Dawn and for divinatory and meditation purposes this seems to be the best system. However, other Tarot trumps have been assigned to different positions in other systems, and I have very successfully used an entirely different set of associations for healing.

Where this form of divination is so powerful is that you can visualise the powers of the sephiroth in the appropriate colours as beams of light as you follow the pathways in your mind to the ultimate goal.

As well as creating a powerful divination system as Tarot and Kabbalistic wisdom unite, it also allows rehearsal of alternative paths to any goal so that a choice is made on detailed foreknowledge of possible consequences. Readings can either be carried out for yourself or for other people. This method is not a system for weekly use but one that if used once a month, or at the time of major opportunities or crises, can convey not only the changes in circumstances, but the inner movement that may unconsciously modify your path and ultimate goals.

Draw or paint a Tree of Life, using the colours listed below, on stiff white card or have it printed on a cloth. Alternatively make a photocopy of the diagram of the full Tree of Life as shown on page 179 as your path to progress. Some people find it helpful to print a series of diagrams so that they can record each separate reading by marking the chosen spheres with a cross or star and track the alternative paths with different coloured pens. On the diagram of the Tree of Life I have used the more traditional names for each sphere as these are the ones used in more formal books on the Kabbalah. However, for the purpose of divination I have adapted names that reflect the meaning of each sphere. Use either.

- **Sphere 1:** Kether, Unity, is white.
- **Sphere 2:** Chokmah, Wisdom, is silver or grey.
- **Sphere 3:** Binah, Understanding, is black.
- **Sphere 4:** Chesed, Mercy, is blue.
- **Sphere 5:** Geburah, Judgement, is red.

- **Sphere 6:** Tiphareth, Beauty, is yellow.
- **Sphere 7:** Netzach, Emotions, is green.
- **Sphere 8:** Hod, Intellect, is orange.
- **Sphere 9:** Yesod, Instincts, is purple.
- **Sphere 10:** Malkuth, the Material World, is brown.

The Kabbalistic Divinatory System

In this method you will use the Minor Arcana cards, excluding the Court cards, to determine your path. Your forty Minor Arcana Ace to Ten cards correspond to the ten sephiroth of the Tree of Life. You can tell the emphasis of the reading by the predominant suit or suits. If you draw more than one card of the same number, you can tell by the sphere it relates to the aspects that are important and you may need to perhaps return to the sphere by a different route.

Keep the Major Arcana cards in a separate pile for use on the Tree.

- Shuffle the forty cards and place them face down.
- Pick three or more cards if necessary to give you a total of three spheres. If you do select three or four of the same card number in consecutive turns, meditate on the cards and sphere colour after your reading (see Chapter 8 on the Tarot and Psychic Development). But pick another card until you have three different numbers, so that you can achieve your three separate spheres.
- Focus on each card in turn, asking silently if it is the one chosen to guide you. Take as long as you need for this and turn the cards over one at a time.
- Look at your first card and place it on the sephira of the same number on your chart.
- Pick the second and then the third. The actual card meanings may shed light on the situation.
- Look first at the separate spheres and combine the

general template meaning with your own intuitive feel. The fact that a system has profound roots should not deter anyone from using it as a personal tool for exploration.

- The first card you selected represents the current situation or urgent question and will include all the past influences and circumstances that have led to the present position. Some of these may have been unconscious but can with effort and intuition be brought to the surface, acknowledged and so lose any hidden powers to hinder or hold back progress.

- The second card represents the optimum immediate gain possible given the present situation, the events moving into your life and your reaction to these events.

- The third card is your ultimate long-term goal, either for your whole life or a particular aspect. Do not be surprised if the issue and answer is contained in the same sphere.

- Next study the pathways. Each pathway between spheres offers gains and losses, sacrifices and opportunities and so you can decide which is the best way forward. This is where your Major Arcana comes into play.

- You may need to travel by more than one path to link your spheres. Use your Major Arcana cards on their pathways (correspondences are given on pages 193–204).

- Read these paths as staging points on a journey linking all the places. If there are alternative routes, try one or two before settling on one, unless the way seems instantly clear. The first choice of route that comes spontaneously is usually dictated by your inner wisdom.

- Place each of the appropriate cards from the Major Arcana on the possible pathways in turn, seeing how the cards link with each other, any possible conflicts and visualise each as a messenger, with words for you that will explain and also challenge. If the same sphere does appear more than once ask why you need to return to it and if you take a different pathway is the second more fulfilling albeit more demanding?

The Sephiroth

THE FIRST LEVEL OF THE TREE

The First and Top Level is often called the Supernal or Supraconscious Realm, representing aspects of the Godhead, abstract thought and higher consciousness beyond human intellect.

It corresponds with the suit of Wands/Staves, the element of Fire and the Kings in the Tarot.

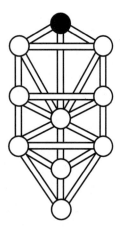

Kether: Unity (Number One)

This is the *prima mobile*, the Great Creator, the Godhead who is beyond all form or tangible existence. Kether lies on the middle pillar of the Tree of Life. Many cultures refer to an original creative or undifferentiated life force, from which all life, positive and negative, good and evil, emanated.

Kether can be regarded as ultimate union with the universe. It is symbolised in mystical tradition by the heavenly Androgyne (male and female united in one), and represents a state of mystical Transcendence and union with the Supreme. The soul which achieves this sphere achieves unity with God.

In everyday terms, Kether can indicate that any decisions are far-reaching, that there are no limits to possible achievement and happiness, and that all the aspects of your life will fuse together. Rise above any pettiness or unworthy thoughts and look to the long-term aim.

In terms of spiritual development, Kether represents ultimate enlightenment and a harmony of mind, body and spirit. It can be visualised as a beam of light coming from the cosmos and returning to it.

Its **colour** is pure white.
Its **key words** are unity, union, pure consciousness, the manifestation, beginning, source.
Its **virtue** or positive aspect is actualisation or attainment

and its **vice** or negative aspect is dissipation or non-achievement.

Chokmah or Hockmah: Wisdom (Number Two)

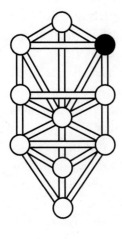

The second emanation on the Tree of Life is linked with the Great Father, the giver of the spark of life, the progenitor and ultimate phallic symbol and so is the realm of the perfect qualities of initiating life, the wisdom of the ages and accumulated knowledge. It is the creative Divine Word of Genesis, the force behind everything positive and dynamic, the impulse which originates action.

It can indicate strongly 'life-giving' and energising sides of both men and women. This is the sphere of conscious wisdom and initiative, the manifestation of the formless creative power into the yang form of positivity, confidence, energy and knowledge, tempered by tradition.

In everyday terms, the card Chokmah represents initiating new ventures and bringing into actuality plans and dreams. Success and achievement must be tempered by idealism and altruism and, where you are in a position of strength, you should use it to achieve a worthwhile aim without hurting others. If you are uncertain, look for the answer from a wise person or written source of wisdom.

In spiritual terms this sphere represents the archetypal animus, so that creativity and the natural desire for achievement are free from materialistic taints and knowledge is a path to enlightenment, not an end in itself.

Its **colour** is silver-grey, a combination of the white of Kether and the black of Binah.

Its **key words** are pure creative energy, life force, the wellspring, light, innovation and initiation based on wisdom and strength.

Its **virtue** or positive aspect is an outpouring of energy and the negative aspect or **vice** is destructiveness.

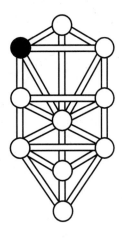

Binah: Understanding (Number Three)

The third emanation is identified with the Great Mother in all her forms. She is the Womb of new life, the life-bearer and transformer of the creative spark of Chokmah into practical form within time and space. Binah is the Great Sea, the primordial great waters of Genesis which were inert but which contained in potential all life. Binah represents the anima, femininity and especially motherhood, nurturing, understanding, self-sacrifice, unconditional love and fertility of spirit.

In everyday terms Binah represents the opportunity and need to accept others with all their faults, to empathise without the desire to possess or manipulate those who are vulnerable and to relate to others, rather than pursuing a separate course. Above all it involves giving birth to ideas within the limitations of the real world so that creation takes a tangible form.

On a spiritual level, Binah is the striving to union with the souls and hearts of others, of giving oneself whole-heartedly to fellow beings, understanding human frailty and bringing joy and fertility in their highest forms.

Her **colour** is black.
Key words include acceptance, limitation, form, constraint, incarnation, fate, time, space, natural law, the womb and gestation, enclosure, fertility, mother, weaving and spinning, death (return to the womb).
The **positive aspect** is abundance and the **negative aspect** is secretiveness.

Daath

There is an invisible sephira below Chokmah and Binah, sometimes called Daath or Knowledge of the Shadow that corresponds with the concept of hidden aspects of the universe that cannot be expressed in words, because they contain the essence of life and death itself.

Daath has no manifest qualities and cannot be invoked directly. It is not used for divinatory purposes. It is also known as the Abyss, the great gulf that separates the ideal from the actual, the infinite from the finite, and divine consciousness from human consciousness.

Its **colour** is grey.
Its **key words** include mystery, abyss, hole, tunnel, gateway, doorway, black hole, vortex.

THE SECOND LEVEL OF THE TREE

This also contains three sephiroth and begins in the world where archetypes are manifest in action and experience. They mirror the higher realms to some extent. This is known as the Realm of the Soul. In this second triangle, form is imposed on what is formless and substance given to ideas.

The two opposing principles, Chesed and Geburah, lower reflections of Chokmah and Binah, control the interplay of creation and destruction in life. They are balanced by the sixth sephira, Tiphareth, the reflection of Kether, the beauty and harmony of ordered nature and the energy of the life force. It is said that Tiphareth is the highest realm attainable by the human mind in its normal state of consciousness.

It corresponds with Cups or Chalices, the Queens and the element of Water in the Tarot.

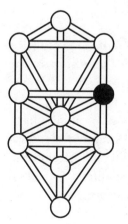

Chesed: Mercy (Number Four)

The fourth emanation is identified with the ruler (but not Creator) of the manifest universe and represents peace, stability, love, awareness and mercy. It is the ruler who commands by example and love, not fear and coercion, the force that systematically builds up and organises the creative growth processes. It is not a weak sephira, but its power is rooted in quiet strength and understanding of a wide perspective and in persuasion.

In the everyday world Chesed represents a gentle, but wise response to any conflict or challenge, showing understanding of the motives and weaknesses of others and not descending to power-seeking or revenge. In the long-term forbearance and dignity will have far more effect than anger and threats.

Any decisions should be carefully considered and based on persuasion and sometimes compromise, not capitulation.

In the spiritual sphere Chesed advises mercy, forgiveness of oneself and others and a move towards understanding the wisdom of letting natural justice and natural karma take its course.

Its **colour** is blue.

Its **key words** include vision, wise authority, leading by example, justice, inspiration, patience, persuasion, spiritual love and vision, altruism and forgiveness.

Its **virtue** is humility and its **vice** self-righteousness.

Geburah: Judgement (Number Five)

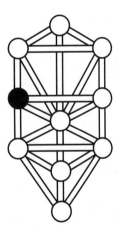

The fifth emanation on the Tree of Life and the alter ego of Chesed, Geburah represents Severity and Justice. The destructive forces of the sphere of Geburah are intended to have a purging, cleansing effect on the universe and destroys what Chesed has created when its day is done.

Geburah represents the Warrior God aspect of the wise ruler who applies discipline and precision in governing the cosmos and removes unwanted or unnecessary elements after their usefulness has passed.

In the everyday world, Geburah represents sacrifice in the most positive sense of giving up the unfruitful or redundant, the sacrificial, cleansing fires that burn in the great solar festivals throughout the world. It is also the determination not to compromise on basic principles or to allow injustices to prevail where others would be hurt. A particular course may seem hard and require great courage, but it is the way to real fulfilment and success.

In the spiritual sphere, Geburah requires the highest standards with self as well as others, accepting no excuses for being less than ethical and moral, an old-fashioned concept but one which demands that only when we have judged ourselves can we judge others.

Its **colour** is red.
Its **key words** include justice, retribution (revenge taken not in the heat of anger but calculated redress of what is necessary), severity, necessary destruction, loyalty and persistence.
Its **virtue** is courage and its **vice** is cruelty.

Tiphareth: Beauty (Number Six)

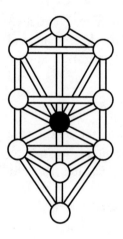

This sphere on the central pillar of the Tree links and harmonises Mercy (Chesed) and Judgement (Geburah), higher on the Tree. It is said to be the sphere of the Self, poised between the world of the spirit and the material world, just as Binah is the greater Self.

In the everyday world, Tiphareth stands for being true to one's own essential self and beliefs, of treading what is called the beauty way, giving and receiving joy, maintaining serenity and not being swayed by either sentiment or the pressures imposed by others. It is an assurance that a person is on the right track, no matter what others say, and that perseverance will assure happiness.

As a spiritual quality, Tiphareth represents the inner world of harmony that is free from the approval or pressures of others to conform to material standards of what is of value.

Its **colour** is yellow.
The **key words** include harmony, reconciliation, peacemaking, self-awareness, balance, wholeness, clear identity. Its **virtue** is integrity and its **vice** is over-concern with outward appearance.

THE THIRD REALM OF THE TREE

This triangle extends towards the roots of the Tree. This is the realm of the Personality and links the material world below expressed in Malkuth with the human personality which aspires upwards through the realms of soul and spirit. Here Netzach and Hod, lower reflections of Chesed and Geburah, represent respectively attraction and cohesion, and flux and change, balanced by Yesod who stands for stability within change through regulated cycles. It corresponds with Swords, the Knights and the element of Air in the Tarot.

Netzach: Emotions (Number Seven)

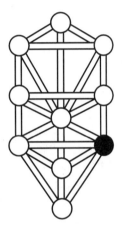

The seventh emanation on the Tree of Life, Netzach is regarded as the sphere of artistic creativity, subjectivity and the emotions, a very clear contrast to the corresponding sphere of Hod, which represents intellect and rational thought.

This forms part of the human sphere and so is the realm of empathy and an intuititive understanding of the feelings of others. Inspiration is the fount of this sphere, whether in using artistic expression or speaking from the heart.

In the everyday sphere, Netzach deals with feelings and intuition. Any response, whether to opportunity or to challenge, should take into account less tangible factors. The inner voice that speaks from the heart can be the most valuable indicator of the best path, as it can access information not known by the conscious sphere. An instant response may be the correct one before doubts and the opinions of others cloud the issue.

In the spiritual realms Netzach is the sudden moment of illumination, the answer that comes unbidden to a question hardly formulated and is implicated in all forms of psychic and spiritual development.

Netzach's **colour** is green.
The **key words** include passion, pleasure, sensual beauty, love, excitement, desire, affection and sympathy.
Its **virtue** is empathy and its **vice** excess of emotion.

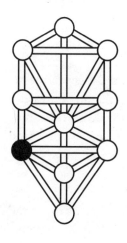

Hod: Intellect (Number Eight)

Hod represents logic, order, rational thought and structure, especially in connection with the human mind. Hod is careful planning, assessment of what is known and deductions made within certain parameters.

In the everyday world, Hod puts forward the logical, ordered approach, following each step and checking for any possible errors. It advocates a cautious, measured response, using head rather than heart.

In the spiritual realms Hod represents acquired knowledge and recognised expertise, and advocates learning as the basis for spiritual advancement.

Its **colour** is orange.

Its **key words** are glory, splendour, abstraction, communication, clear conceptualisation, logic and rule-keeping.

Its **virtue** is truthfulness and its **vice** dishonesty and pedantry.

Yesod: Instincts (Number Nine)

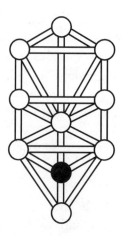

The ninth emanation is sometimes known as the 'animal soul', the seat of instincts, especially sexual and procreative ones. Yesod is the sphere of physical fertility whether in deeds or in the act of ejaculation, pregnancy and birth. It is also source of physical desires, whether for sexual or oral satisfaction through food, drink, smoking, drugs or indulgences of desires for physical comfort and stimulation. The higher instincts in this unconscious realm represent the search for meaning, beauty and grace, mingled and sometimes in conflict with the animal energies for personal satisfaction.

Yesod is the spout for the waters from on high, the channel between vital Divine energy and the earth or earthly humanity, in terms of psychology, the sphere of the unconscious mind.

In the everyday world, Yesod appears when there is a choice between personal gratification and restraint, seeing through the imagination and through divination, possibilities from within the unconscious psyche. There is the opportunity for either noble or baser actions which may offer instant gratification.

In the spiritual sense, Yesod has a dual, deeper meaning, connected with the primitive call of the unseen world. It is associated with the astral plane, with dreams and divination, and if one can rise above illusion, a connection with the powerful mysteries of the universe.

Its **colour** is purple.

The **key words** include perception, healing of the mind and spirit, imagination, images reflected from the psyche, the unconscious, instinct, life cycles as mirrored by the moon and tides, and secrets.

Its **virtue** is focused imagination and its **vice** self-gratification.

THE FOURTH LEVEL OF THE TREE

This is the realm of the Material World and contains a single sephira, Malkuth, the world of the earth, the physical body and brain of humankind, but which is also, it is said, at the same time the entire manifest kingdom of God, the Word made flesh. This corresponds with the suit of Pentacles or Discs, with the Pages and with the Earth element in the Tarot.

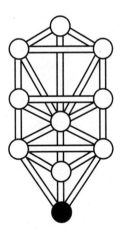

Malkuth: The Material World (Number Ten)

The tenth emanation is associated with the immediate environment, the plane of physical reality and its connections with the underworld and mortality. Sometimes it is called the lower unconscious mind where we link with the Earth.

All 'inner journeys of consciousness' begin symbolically in Malkuth and this is therefore an important sphere for the start of any journey and a reminder of our roots and our connection with the Earth. It may appear when the issue is one of survival and talks about an instinctive gut response as opposed to intuition or logic. As a sphere it holds great physical strength for regeneration that can be translated as endurance or a sudden surge of energy to fight back, not necessarily in a physical sense, but as a mental response to an actual crisis or challenge.

In the everyday world, Malkuth says that you should return to roots whatever the issue. If a reversal of fortune or a new path means that you have to go back to basics, use its power to assess the priorities, including material ones and leave behind the illusions and even spiritual aspirations. It is by no means an inferior sephira, for without the Earth we would have no roots.

On a spiritual level, Malkuth represents the reality principle, the point at which the world cannot be ignored but must be conquered with all its physical and material limitations. Malkuth also stands for a kinship with all life, animal, plant and stone as well as human. It is the roots of the Tree of Life.

Its **colour** is brown.

Its **key words** include reality, healing of the body, physical matter, the natural world, practicality, solidity, death and incarnation and return to the Earth.

Its **virtue** is connectedness with all life and its **vice** materialism or inertia.

The Tarot Pathways

Each sephira is linked to others by pathways that can either ascend or descend. I have described the paths of descent, but for the upward path the energies simply flow the other way. The pathways are especially important since alternative routes may involve different choices. Sometimes the most direct or easiest path may not necessarily be the best, but the decision is your own. Each pathway has positive and negative connotations. Although the Kabbalah is a powerful spiritual path, Tarot divination can also be used to ask and resolve issues about everyday life. This more earthly application should not be seen as less worthy, since the Kabbalah embraces every aspect of the human condition. Sometimes the pathways are numbered 1 to 22, but in most interpretations they begin at 11, carrying on from the numbering of the sephiroth.

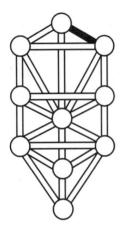

PATH 11: THE FOOL

Links spheres 1 to 2 Kether to Chokmah, known as the Scintillating Path or the Path of Fiery Potential, the first outpouring of light from Kether and pure potential so that anything is possible in the innocent, unspoilt Divine Child, the Fool.

The Hebrew letter *Aleph* א is assigned to Path 11 and the Fool. Aleph means ox or bull and in many traditional creation myths the Divine Cow is seen as the source of life. The bull was also used as a symbol for God and represents creative and undifferentiated force, the pure life force and spark of life that permeates all animate and inanimate forms.

So the path of the Fool is the great step into the unknown made in pure faith, leaving behind logic, doubts, restrictions and material trappings. At any level it is the path of limitless possibility – and the only drawback is hesitation.

Trust is the key word.

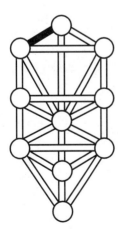

PATH 12: THE MAGICIAN

Links spheres 1 to 3, Kether to Binah, known as the Transparent Path or the Path of Visions. This is the way of the visionary, the true clairvoyant who carries within him or herself the power to see what is of worth and ways of developing the untapped potential in us all.

It is assigned the Hebrew letter *Beth* ב which means house and so is the vessel of life, the bodily house of the spirit and so its means of expression as well as its physical limits.

So the path of the Magician at any level is the way of

inspired and focused action, undaunted by constraints of the here and now, and the only drawback is in lacking the will to bring the vision into actuality.

Clarity is the key word.

PATH 13: THE HIGH PRIESTESS

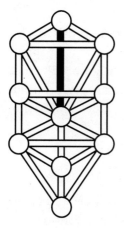

Links the spheres 1 to 6, Kether to Tiphareth, and is known as the Uniting Path or the Way of Enlightenment. This is the way linking the seen with the unseen, the known with the unknown, sometimes called the Dark Night of the Soul because it is the direct path across Daath or the Abyss, from light through darkness into light again and so is a path involving courage and faith that if followed will lead to an understanding of the diversity of life.

The Hebrew letter *Gimel* ג means camel, a means of crossing vast tracts of barren land. So the path of the High Priestess is the central unwavering way between the pillars of light and darkness, and the Source of Light. At any level this talks about the reconciliation of opposites and the acceptance that there cannot always be uncertainties and the only drawback is doubt.

Acceptance is the key word.

PATH 14: THE EMPRESS

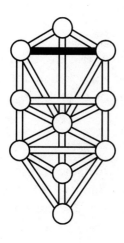

Links the spheres 2 to 3, Chokmah with Binah, known as the Path of Illumination and Generation, of the primal union of Chokmah and Binah, bridging, as the Empress, the male and female aspects, the animus and anima within ourselves, in the birth of a child.

The Hebrew letter of Empress is *Daleth* ד, the door, and so it is that abundance, new life and light are created by the passing through the doorway between male and female and coming together in a new, integrated life form. At any level, the Empress pathway is one of creative imagination, of giving freely and of fertility. The only drawback is when one aspect swamps the other.

Integration is the key word.

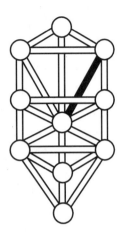

PATH 15: THE EMPEROR

Links the spheres 2 to 6, Chokmah and Tiphareth, the Way of Organisation and Law, the manifestation of the Word in actuality within the framework of the here and now, touched with harmony and modified by the experience of crossing the Abyss.

The Hebrew letter is *Heh* ה, a window, that is also related to the Universal Life Force and so the light shines now not in an undifferentiated form, but powerfully in a controlled way. At any level, the Emperor's way is one of order, structure, organised thought and action, and its only drawback is if it becomes too rigid.

Power is the key word of the Emperor.

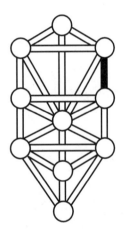

PATH 16: THE HIEROPHANT

Links the spheres 2 to 4, Chokmah and Chesed, known as the Path of Quiet Wisdom, the eternal bridge to Paradise, the state of stillness in which the small voice of calm, the inner voice, may be heard and can act as a guide and certainty through even tumultuous times.

The Hebrew letter is *Vau* ו, the nail, a symbol of connection in this case between Divine Wisdom and Divine Mercy. At any level the Hierophant is the mediator and also transmitter of spiritual knowledge and so the way is one of gentle, considered words and seeking guidance from spiritual sources, the deep unconscious wisdom within as well as external mentors. Its only drawback is if the path is seen as the end and not the means to progress.

Reflection is the key word.

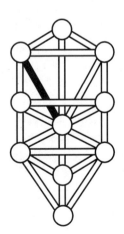

PATH 17: THE LOVERS

Links the spheres 3 to 6, Binah to Tiphareth, the Path of Absorption into Others, the union of Sun and Moon energies, animus and anima, conscious and unconscious powers, which are absorbed in the Primal Waters, the Womb of Binah, and re-formed, so that we are not longer alone, but connecting through love with those who complement and complete the separate self.

The Hebrew letter is *Zain* ז which means sword, the sword which can cut through false attachments, but which also warns of the need when crossing the Abyss for the separate person in a sense to die in order to be joined with its alter ego as well as its own shadow self. At any level the path of the Lovers steers us towards the experience of sharing our needs and aims with those who follow a similar path, drawing strength from them and offering it in return. The only drawback is in endowing others with our own faults that we deny in ourselves.

Kinship is the key word.

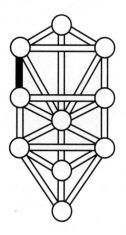

PATH 18: THE CHARIOT

Links spheres 3 to 5, Binah to Geburah, the Path of Formation by Experience, the tempering flame, whereby good and bad situations we encounter mould us into our unique and ever-changing self, as we experience challenging paths and fresh perspectives.

The Hebrew letter is *Cheth* ח, a fence or enclosure, which talks about the structuring of the spiritual by events as life evolves, and the need to channel and rein in any tendencies that deviate from the personal evolutionary path. There is also the suggestion of agriculture, the need to plant seeds that will grow in the future. At any level the Chariot is the path of learning from experience and realising that travelling what may not be an easy way will bear fruit. The only drawback is if change becomes an end in itself, rather than for a purpose.

Change is the key word.

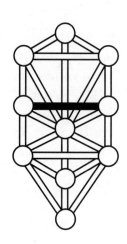

PATH 19: STRENGTH

Links spheres 4 to 5, Chesed to Geburah, the Path of Gentle Power, the way of blessings, as Divine Mercy and Divine Severity are joined not by force or brutality, but the gentle Strength, that can in the Tarot card imagery control a lion.

The Hebrew letter is *Teth* ט, a serpent curved into a circle, the celestial serpent which forms the circle of the twelve signs of the zodiac or the alchemical *ourobos* who swallows his own tail and therefore signifies life without end, perpetually restoring and nourishing itself – the Lion in some Tarot packs has a serpent's tail. The link with the serpent in its heavenly aspects shows that there must be a balance between the instinctual and spiritual process so that we are always led towards the highest possible motive in our actions. At any level Strength is the path that says that endurance, persistence and self-denial are needed if gentleness is not to degenerate into weakness and therein lies its drawback.

Persistence is the key word.

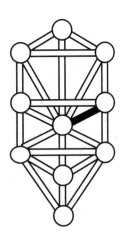

PATH 20: THE HERMIT

Link spheres 4 to 6, Chesed to Tiphareth, the solitary path, the Path of the Inner Flame, that unlike the path of the Lovers, seeks inner harmony and beauty, by renouncing earthly love and pleasures for introspection and inner illumination.

The Hebrew letter is *Yod* י, the smallest letter in the Hebrew alphabet, the hand that extends to other seekers. At any level the path of the Hermit counsels the need to seek inner rather than outer development as, until one is spiritually evolved, it is not possible to reach or teach others.

Introspection is the key word.

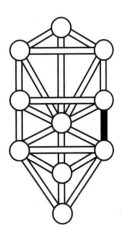

PATH 21: THE WHEEL OF FORTUNE

Links spheres 4 to 7, Chesed and Netzach, the Path of Fate, of adapting to the rise and fall of circumstance, so that emotions and earthly desires are shaped by cause and effect, but do not lose connection with the higher power of love and mercy, wherein forgiveness and acceptance of setbacks as part of one's karma reside. The Sphinx of wisdom on top of the card says that we can change our lives for the better by recourse to the Higher Self, whatever the circumstances.

The Hebrew letter is *Kaph* כ, a cupped hand, but can

also represent an open hand or palm which reflects the processes of alternatively giving and taking, winning and losing, as the Wheel of Life turns. At whatever level, the path of the Wheel is one of reacting positively to any setbacks and aiming for what is of worth that may lie behind material fortune. The only drawback is when someone waits for fate to bring fulfilment and resolution of difficulties, the downside of fortune telling.

Self-control is the key word.

PATH 22: JUSTICE

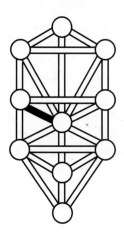

Links the spheres 5 to 6, Geburah to Tiphareth, the Path of Faith and of right thought and action, whereby justice is not rigid or retributive, moderating Geburah or severity with the radiant and harmonious Tiphareth.

The Hebrew letter is *Lamed* ל, an ox-goad. Lamed regulates *Aleph*, the ox or breath of life which is associated with Kether and drives the Divine energy into the dispensation of justice at its most noble, so that people act naturally from good motives and need little goading from outside, thus following universal rather than human-made laws. At any level the path of Justice involves compromise and an allowance of human weakness, while standing firm over what is of worth. The only drawback is if the desire for justice overrides all other aspects of the personality.

Balance is the key word.

PATH 23: THE HANGED MAN

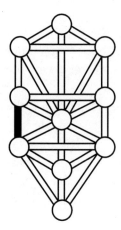

Links spheres 5 to 8, Geburah to Hod, the Path of Surrender and Glory, as the spheres of sacrifice and following the pre-ordained path are joined by the concept of letting go of even the personality in order to reach true spiritual enlightenment.

The Hebrew letter is *Mem* מ, the waters or seas and so it is in the immersion of the soul in these great primordial waters that by the suspension of ordinary consciousness and ordinary activity, the real person can emerge, having shed all the images and illusions, opened to the cosmos. At any level the path of the Hanged Man may involve sacrifice in the short term for greater understanding. The only drawback occurs when the sacrifice is not a worthwhile one.

Surrender is the key word.

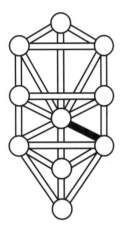

PATH 24: DEATH

Links spheres 6 to 7, Tiphareth to Netzach, the Path of Renewal and Change, examining the role of endings and finiteness and the conflict between survival instincts and the desire for oblivion.

The Death is that of the ego, following the surrender of the previous path and the rebirth of the new self in which the feelings of Netzach are experienced as spiritual joy in Tiphareth.

The Hebrew letter is *Nun* ב, a fish, the life from within the primordial waters of the previous path. The letter also means to sprout or generate and so the concept is one of transformation and life out of death, joy out of sorrow and victory out of surrender. At any level, the path of Death is not one to be feared but as a means of overcoming fears, once the door on what is finished is closed. The only drawback is in the fears that are worse than the actuality.

Life is the key word.

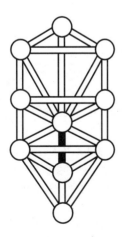

PATH 25: TEMPERANCE

Links spheres 6 to 9, Tiphareth to Yesod, the tentative Path of New Directions and the modification of the inner world as the conscious power and radiant energy of the Sun in Tiphareth illuminates and gives form to the unstructured imaginative and intuitive faculties of the Moon in Yesod.

The Moon represents the personality and the Sun symbolises the Higher Self and so the Higher Self finds expression in the life of the seeker. This is an important card, for the Angel or Goddess of the Rainbow enables truth to be separated from illusion.

The Hebrew letter is *Samekh* ס, a rough stone set up on end, support and so new beliefs and theories are tested as it were against a touchstone and previous apparent certainties modified when illumination is shed upon them. At any level the path of Temperance is one involving the shedding of false illusions to be replaced by a patient groping for the truth and so it is a gradual path involving patience and a slow movement to enlightenment. The only drawback is if what is of worth in the world of imagination is shed.

Patience is the key word.

PATH 26: THE DEVIL

Links spheres 6 to 8, Tiphareth to Hod, the Renovating Path, the path in which the radiance is perceived through the discerning rather than physical eye and material concerns are seen as less worth while than spiritual riches.

The Hebrew letter is *Ayin* ע, eye, the physical eye that sees only the surface, but which if combined with intellect from Hod, penetrates beyond apparent success and riches, from instant satisfaction to a striving after meaning. At any level, the path of the Devil is one of self-gratification and of temptation to settle for second best or success in material terms, perhaps at the sacrifice of principle. The only drawback is if intellectual perceptions block the inner eye so that these temptations are not faced and overcome.

Discernment is the key word.

PATH 27: THE TOWER

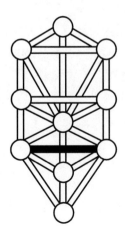

Links spheres 7 to 8, Netzach to Hod, the Tumultuous Path between the cohesion of Netzach and the flux of Hod, so that as with the concepts of the ancient webs of fate, what is created is constantly torn down so that it can be reformed in the light of new events and experience.

The Hebrew letter is *Peh* פ, mouth, from which comes both the breath of life in Netzach and words from Hod – indeed sometimes a lightning flash is seen coming from the mouth of a sage. Prophecy, the spontaneous outpouring of inspired knowledge, is associated with Peh. At any level the path of the Tower is of words that must be spoken that will destroy old conceptions and restrictions to allow new ideas to develop. The only drawback is if the destruction is so great it wilts the shoots of new life.

Communication is the key word.

PATH 28: THE STAR

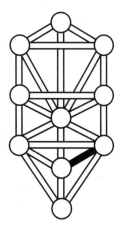

Links spheres 7 to 9, Netzach to Yesod, the Path of Hope and Meditation, that follows the Star to enlightenment and fulfilment, recognising the unique destiny we all have to unfold, guided by the spiritual hunger that drives us, fuelled by the emotions and desires in Netzach and the intuitive wisdom of Yesod.

The Hebrew letter is *Tzaddi* צ, the fish-hook, the means of probing the unconscious waters of the psyche and drawing out what is of substance. The hook also lifts the seeker out of the material world towards the light of the Star which represents true fulfilment. At any level the path of the Star is one of following the path of happiness, by focusing on a single goal that will satisfy the deeper aspects of mind and soul. The only drawback is waiting for the dream to come true by itself.

Ascent is the key word.

PATH 29: THE MOON

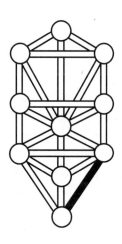

Links the spheres 7 to 10, Netzach to Malkuth, the Secret Path Through the Darkness, as the physical body is awakened fertilised by the psyche. Sleep and dreams are the children of the Moon, as are psychic explorations and these are doorways between the body and other dimensions.

The Hebrew letter is *Qoph* ק, the back of the head, seat of the brain and consciousness, said in esoteric wisdom to connect the higher brain centres and the spinal cord and lower centres of the body, even in sleep. It is important to strengthen the connection between body and soul, rather than deny the importance of the body as the house of the spirit. The five senses and physical sensations are a way of reaching and developing the sixth sense. Spiritual experiences begin in and through the imagination. At any level the path of the Moon is one for trusting dreams, daytime insights and intuitive flashes. The drawback is in spending too long in dreams.

Intuition is the key word.

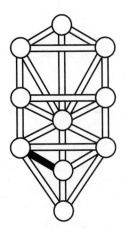

PATH 30: THE SUN

Links spheres 8 to 9, Hod to Yesod, the Path of the Inner Teachers and Guides, between Hod, sephira of knowledge and Yesod, the world of imagination and intuition. It is a path illuminated and empowered by the Sun in its full glory, so that what was hidden is now revealed and dreams have firm foundations.

The Hebrew letter is *Resh* ר, head or face, and there is a link with the Sun who is the brilliant face of the solar system. So conscious thought emanating in the head, fuelled by visionary inspiration, offers a path of discovery and potential fulfilment. At any level the golden path of the Sun clears away both inner and outer obstructions so that we can unfold our innate gifts. The only drawback is in lacking the courage to trust the visions as well as the logic.

Discovery is the key word.

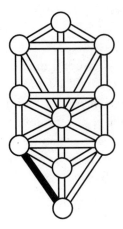

PATH 31: JUDGEMENT

Links spheres 8 to 10, Hod to Malkuth, the Path of Fire or the Perpetual Path, the controlled Fire that burns away dross and refines the Reason and Mind Power of Hod within the material world or earthly body of Malkuth, so that experience is transformed into wise action.

The Hebrew letter is *Shin* ש, a tooth that bites through what is worth consuming to feed the body and spits out what is not of use. The lines on the letter offer the magical significance which is linked with the Spirit descending in tongues of Fire. At any level the path of Judgement is a reminder of cause and effect of earthly action on the spirit and vice versa, and says that the consequences of any action must be weighed up logically. The only drawback is when the controlling Fire becomes all-consuming and reduces the seeker to a state of guilt or helpless anger.

Transformation is the key word.

PATH 32: THE WORLD OR UNIVERSE

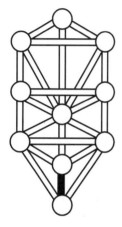

Links spheres 9 to 10, Yesod to Malkuth, the Path of the Sacred Centre or the still point of the Universe which is at the centre of every being. The seven chakras or energy points of the human body are linked with seven planets, circling around the sacred source of life. 'As above, so below' and so the sacred centre within the body is in a sense the purpose and fruition of every quest since it mirrors the cosmos.

The Hebrew letter of this path is *Tau* ת, a seal or witness, expressed in the Tau Cross which, formed like a capital T, is the point where Earth and Heaven meet. There are many complex associations with this symbol that you can read about in the books in the suggested reading list at the back of this book, but the meaning is both boundlessness and completion. At any level the path of the World or Universe promises not the end of endeavour, but an understanding of the point of existence and a way of stepping out of the relentless tread of time. The only drawback is mistaking the inner stillness for inaction.

Perfection is the key word.

Each of these pathways is ultimately a personal journey and the concepts suggested by each card will be modified in each of us by our unique experiences and world view. It would take a lifetime to unravel the profound wisdom behind the Kabbalah and yet we can all gain benefits, even at this rudimentary level, if we trust our innate wisdom and the spiritual bonds we all have with the creator spirit of which we are part.

Lighting up the Tree of Life

Each sephira has a colour. If you have a difficult decision to make it can help to spread out your map of the Tree of Life on the floor or a table and place on each sephira a small candle in a holder. If the holder is broad and fire-proof it should not mark your Tree, but you can use the positions marked by candles without the Tree.

- As you pick a sphere in divination light the candle and sit for a few minutes gazing into it.
- Select your second card and light the candle of that sphere and do the same for the third, sitting quietly looking at your lights.
- When you have decided on your pathway which may involve more than one path between spheres, place the appropriate cards on the path and light small white candles behind them.
- Insight will come in the form of images and words in your mind and when you feel that you understand the message, blow out the candles one by one, beginning with the last one you lit, sending the light to all who need it, not forgetting yourself.

Chapter 10

The Tarot and Numerology

What is Numerology?

In Ancient Egypt and among the Phoenicians, mathematics were the province of a priest–scribe caste which, as they explored the hidden depths of numbers, found rules governing them that related to everyday life. So numbers became intrinsic to magical ritual. Numbers, the mathematicians thought, held the key to everything. The ancient Chinese sages and the Pythagoreans (as the followers of the Greek philosopher Pythagoras were called) attributed certain powers to numbers. One they saw as the source of all numbers and really standing apart from the others. All other numbers were regarded as odd or even, the odd numbers yang, male, positive and dynamic, and even numbers yin, female, negative in the sense of positive and negative poles of electricity and receptive. Each number which was expressed diagramatically, as shown in the example of four below, also has its personal characteristic:

Four, the balanced 'square' number stood for justice.

From these roots sprang the mystical art of gematria or numerology. Gradually mathematicians found that using diagrams for numbers was far too awkward. One solution adopted first by the Hebrews and later by the Greeks was to give each of the letters of their alphabet a numerical value (for more information on this see my book *The Complete Book of Magic and Ritual*, published by Piatkus, 1999).

Tarot cards also have been endowed with numerical significance. There are differences in the numbering of the Major Arcana in that the Fool can be 0, 1 or 22. But the most stable numbering system that has support from many traditional sources is that used in the Rider Waite Tarot and the Universal Waite Tarot. In other packs, Strength at number 8 and Justice at number 11 are sometimes interchanged and the number significance is likewise transposed.

The Ace to Ten Minor Arcana cards have inbuilt numbers which can enrich the meaning and for numerological calculations in general readings you can also count Pages as 4, Knights as 3, Queens as 2 and Kings as 1. These are associated with the four main levels on the Tree of Life, so that for example the Pages represent the fourth and lowest material realm. Pages are likewise linked with the Earth or material element (see Chapter 2 on the Court Cards).

By the same measure Wands/Staves are linked with 1, Cups and Chalices 2, Swords 3 and Pentacles or Discs 4. If you are only using the Minor Arcana or Court cards you thereby still have a wealth of numerical values for calculations.

The Major Arcana and Numbers

0 THE FOOL

Zero is the symbol of time and space without limit, the eternal circle without beginning or end. The Fool represents therefore potential thought and action in the future, as yet unbound by negativity, the source of Light or the Godhead. This heralds an unknown but potentially exciting future; therefore in any reading this optimistic card will give unrestricted energy to the other cards and prompt a step into the unexplored.

1 THE MAGICIAN

Number 1 is unity, the Word or Logos, the first manifestation of creative light that will multiply into millions of unique parts, each separate and yet containing the power of the first. It is associated with the One God, the All-Father, the oneness of all humankind and the separate self. The Magician is in any reading a card of power, to make things happen and to innovate while preserving the essence and originality of the instigator.

2 THE HIGH PRIESTESS

Number 2 is the symbol of duality, the Mother/anima principle, separate from the Father/animus contained in Number 1. Number 2 contains both complementary and opposing forces of polarity, light and darkness, as symbolised by the Celtic Oak and Holly Kings, the Waxing and Waning Year, who fought at the equinoxes. The High Priestess, the Virgin, represents the balance so that one force does not annihilate the other.

3 THE EMPRESS

Number 3 is the number of a trinity – father, mother and child, Father, Son and Holy Spirit, and the Triple Goddess of the Celts, maiden, mother and crone. The sacred triangle is a form representing the Eternal especially in Ancient Egypt.

Three is a number of fertility, creation and also balance, and so this card in a reading will herald new beginnings and births of all kinds, spiritual and mental as well as physical and of integration.

4 THE EMPEROR

Number 4 is the number of the square, the physical and material world, and is said to be the most stable of all numbers, with crosses having four arms symbolising Spirit, the vertical line penetrating the horizontal Matter. This is the Father principle within time, space and matter. The Emperor card in a reading represents order, stability and material achievement but always controlled power.

5 THE HIEROPHANT

Number 5 is a very spiritual number, representing the quintessence, the fifth element created from the other four that unifies Earth, Air, Fire and Water and is itself greater. The pentagram is a symbol of great spiritual and magical power, like Man extending his head or single point upwards to the heavens. So the Hierophant represents the greatest good and recourse to our higher nature. It is also associated with health and healing.

6 THE LOVERS

Number 6 is of great mystical significance since it represents the six days taken to create the Earth and the six-pointed Seal of Solomon, a form with pagan as well as formal religious associations as a symbol of perfection and integration. Opposites merge as complementary forces within its interconnecting triangles. The Lovers is a harmonising card in any reading, especially those linked with love matters – but the emphasis is on spiritual not just earthly love.

7 THE CHARIOT

Number 7 is the number of perfection, the most sacred of all numbers, a combination of the sacred Three representing Spirit and the four elements of nature, manifesting God in every aspect of creation. To the Ancient Egyptians seven was a symbol of eternal life. The seventh day was holy because on this day God rested and so came the Commandment to keep the Sabbath day holy. There were also the seven ancient planets which were believed to endow Man with their qualities as he descended to Earth through the spheres. The Chariot is a card of mastery over one's actions and taking control of personal destiny.

8 STRENGTH

Number 8 is sometimes called the Way of the Serpent as man travels on the road to wisdom by weaving through different choices and polarities. This path is mirrored in the shape of the number. As the highest single even number, it represents balance and this path is also one associated with prosperity and authority, especially matters of justice with its emphasis on cause and effect. So this card in a reading, though it achieves its effect not by force, is nevertheless one where quiet determination will overcome quite heavy opposition, especially in matters of principle or financial survival.

9 THE HERMIT

Number 9 is primarily the number of initiation, both in religious and magical rituals where actions are carried out nine times as a sign of perfection and completion. As the last of the single numbers, it brings the sequence to a close – for after it there are no new numbers, merely combinations. It is poised on the edge of the units and double figure numbers, as the Hermit with his lamp walks between worlds. In a reading, it can mark a deeper level, whether of commitment or understanding, since it is the symbol of that which brings things to an end and prepares for a new manifestation. The Hermit is a gateway to the unknown, although it is not the abandoned leap of the Fool but a cautious groping through the mists of the psyche.

10 THE WHEEL OF FORTUNE

Number 10 is the number formed from the 0 of unmanifested force which has now evolved through the other nine numbers. The 1 marks the next and higher stage. It is a number associated with Isis and Osiris, the 1 and 0. Osiris was ritually killed and dismembered by his brother Set and re-formed and brought back from the dead by Isis his sister/wife, the mother goddess in the annual Corn God sacrifice/rebirth, so that the Nile would flood each year and fertilise the soil. So the Wheel of Fortune is seen not as random fate but part of a continuing cycle of rise followed by fall, joy by sorrow and back again, and this is of prime significance in a reading.

11 JUSTICE

Number 11, like 22, is a sacred number in both Pythagorean and Hebrew numerology and even when numbers are reduced to single digits for numerological calculations, sometimes keeps its forms. Known as the number of the Visionary, it represents illumination, idealism, insight into the unspoken motives and intentions of others, and seeker of the secrets of the cosmos. Justice is therefore mediated by insight and an awareness of motive and the whole picture. Memory, experience and perspective has passed into this symbol of new beginnings and so choices are wise ones. In a reading, Justice is linked by its number to high ideas and moral questions rather than legal matters.

12 THE HANGED MAN

Number 12 is the number of measure and time: think of the twelve months of the year and the twelve signs of the zodiac. It is a number of duality with the two separated from the one, yet united. So the Hanged Man takes the step out of time in order that he may conquer it. In the agricultural festivals of the world, the Corn God must step out of the Wheel of the Year so that the cycle can continue. The Hanged Man, through association with his number, in readings suggests that it may be necessary to push to the limits to overcome fears and a repetitive cycle or situation that may seem fruitless in one's own life.

13 DEATH

Number 13 is mistakenly seen as unlucky because of its association with transformation and in ancient societies such as Egypt was said to hold great power if truths could be confronted. It is the eternal cycle of beginnings, fruition and endings, followed by new beginnings, often encapsulated in the image of the Spring Equinox where the ancient King of the Light, the Oak King, equalled, fought and overcame his brother the Holly King of the dark half of the year. But this was not regarded as a once and for all victory and once the Longest Day passed the Holly King would gain in strength until he equalled and overcame his brother at the Autumn Equinox.

So the Death card, in its number, speaks of the futility of fighting inevitable change and promises new happiness once the reality of the creation–destruction cycle is accepted, not feared.

14 TEMPERANCE

Number 14 is a card of mental faculties and balance and not emotions, as expressed in its 4. The practical foundation is extended to stability of the mind, of weighing up situations and people, not coldly, but using reason and compassion rather than sentiment. As a compound of seven it represents the second stage of completion and so in a reading Temperance advises weighing up all the circumstances and making a considered rather than an instant decision or plan.

15 THE DEVIL

Number 15 takes the human rather than divine aspect of the Hierophant and can represent the creation of false ideals and principles or even attachments that have become elevated and so in a sense are imprisoning. But the key is within ourselves and so this is a card of being aware that for the best motives we may idealise people or situations. By ignoring natural and inevitable failings in ourselves and others we may experience unnecessary disillusion when our idols have feet of clay or we deviate from our principles.

16 THE TOWER

Number 16 is a very positive number, rooted in the 6 of love and though this number was depicted by the Chaldeans as a King falling from a tower rent by lightning, nevertheless it represents the release of the flow of love and feelings. The cards says that any area of life where there has been seeming destruction, loss or stagnation, forms the foundations for a new, much stronger relationship or situation, based on all the experience gained through earlier pain or problems.

17 THE STAR

Number 17 expresses the guiding light of the Star of the Magi, that leads to a path of quietness. So the Star in its number, in any reading, expresses the quiet certainty that you are on the right path and that you should not be pressurised by any who seek to hurry you or to cast doubts that you have made wise choices.

18 THE MOON

Number 18 is that of the exploration of secret, inner worlds, containing in the shape of the 8 the Way of the Serpent, the path that must weave through many illusions and false options, and make choices that may be difficult. It is a number of secrets to be unfolded and also those to be kept. The Moon card then is one that says it is important to tread carefully, 'tread softly for you tread on my dreams', the old saying goes and that is what you must do as hidden matters unfold in their own time.

19 THE SUN

Number 19 is a number of attainment as the quest of the 9 reaches the completion of another cycle, as clarity breaks through uncertainty and any unresolved matters move towards fruition. Both number and card are the light at the end of any tunnel and recognition of achievement by others, as well as perhaps long-awaited happiness before the Sun cycle of the year is completed.

20 JUDGEMENT

This is the number of unity as the two separate 10s are united, so that God and Man, Man and Nature, Body and Soul become one. Judgement therefore is softened by its number, suggesting the reconciling of difficulties, the end of alienation and the resolution of any differences in a way that will bring both parties together. In a reading Judgement can finally put aside doubts, regrets and bitterness, and herald that new understanding will explain and end a negative situation or resentment that may have dragged on too long.

21 THE UNIVERSE OR WORLD

After the unity and stability of the previous card, new beginnings and a new cycle move into action and the 1 strikes out from the stability of the 2, but this time much wiser, more certain and with a real chance of success and happiness as you move into challenges previously unimaginable. It indicates you can proceed with confidence and should broaden your options.

22 THE NUMBER OF THE EAGLE

If your pack has either the World or the Fool at this position, it is a card of great power, since 22 is considered to be the most perfect number totally balanced. It is said to represent the master builders of society, shapers of policy, global thinkers, the coming together of reason and intuition, logic and feeling, vision and practicality, energy and compassion. It offers, then, potential for achievement both in the world's terms and in spiritual evolution.

Using Numbers in Tarot Readings

As well as using the separate numbers for individual cards, you can also obtain information about the overall direction of a reading by adding together all the numbers of the chosen cards and reducing them to a single digit.

The numerological method is very good at revealing unexpected factors or opportunities that are moving into your life in the days or weeks following the reading (see also Chapter 5). The Number of Fate can help you to plan new directions, avoid potential hazards and can bring hope even to a seemingly stagnant or intractable situation.

You can find this Number of Fate by adding together all the Major Arcana numbers, plus the numbers of the Minor Arcana and the value of King, Queen, etc., ignoring the suit values. Then reduce this number to a single digit: for example, if you selected The Magician, Six of

Pentacles, King of Cups, Seven of Swords, the Hierophant and the Star, their values would be:

1 + 6 + 1 + 7 + 5 + 17 which adds up to 37
Add the remaining digits: 3 + 7 = 10
Finally 1 + 0 = 1, making the Number of Fate 1

In a relationship spread using only the Court cards you can add together both suit and card values and again obtain a single number that will reveal the unexpected influences of an outsider or external factor upon the dynamics of the relationship that can help to give a fresh perspective or suggest ways of counteracting perhaps unwarranted interference.

Key Words and Potential for each Number

The meanings of the individual numbers vary from system to system and also according to the context in which the numbers are used.

1 THE NUMBER OF THE INNOVATOR
The number 1 is the number of the initiator of action, the pioneer and the leader, with individuality, enthusiasm, drive, assertiveness, strength, boundless energy and originality. As the overall number in a reading, it predicts the unexpected and the original solution.

2 THE NUMBER OF THE NEGOTIATOR
The number 2 is the number of the mediator who can see both sides of any question and weld together disparate elements. As an overall number in a reading, it augers success in partnerships of all kinds as long as you are prepared to adapt.

3 THE NUMBER OF THE CREATOR
The number 3 is the number of the joy-bringer and the visionary. As an overall number in a reading, it says that

the more you give a situation now, the greater your long-term rewards.

4 THE NUMBER OF THE REALIST

The number 4 is the number of the doer rather than the thinker whose ideas work in practice rather than on paper. As an overall number in your reading, it says that if you can work within constraints, you will turn the situation to your advantage.

5 THE NUMBER OF THE COMMUNICATOR

The number 5 is the number of the explorer and the investigator, searching new fields of knowledge as well as distant places. As an overall number in your reading, it indicates you should question decisions that seem narrow-minded or unwise.

6 THE NUMBER OF THE INTEGRATOR

The number 6 is the number of the faithful and loving heart and the protector of the weak. As an overall number in a reading, 6 says that you may need to provide emotional security for others and in doing so gain personal happiness.

7 THE NUMBER OF THE MYSTIC

The number 7 is the number of the wise one who respects the spirit rather than the letter of tradition. As an overall number of your reading, it says that you must listen to your dreams for the answer to an everyday dilemma.

8 THE NUMBER OF THE ENTREPRENEUR

The number 8 is the number of the speculator who nevertheless makes decisions on logic and facts as well as inspiration. As an overall number in your reading, it indicates that if financial opportunities are planned meticulously they will bear not only financial fruit, but also personal satisfaction.

9 **THE NUMBER OF THE CRUSADER**

The number 9 is the number of the seeker of the elusive Grail who refuses to be silenced if the cause is just. If this is your overall number in a reading, you may be moved to defend someone or something close to your heart. However, in your crusade, you should avoid the intolerant attitude you despise in others.

An Options Spread Reading – full pack, Major Arcana or full Minor Arcana

This is a very useful spread if you have two possible paths to follow and cannot decide which is best. It uses the first card you pick to ask a specific question or identify an area of concern. You then add three cards below the left and three cards below the right of the top card to make two alternative paths as shown in the layout below. Decide before you deal which path will apply to each question. It can be used for any issue where alternatives are involved, but is especially effective where numerology is being added for extra information.

ANDY'S NUMEROLOGICAL READING

Andy worked as a presenter in local radio, but was desperate to make a big breakthrough with a London-based station. However, his show tapes were ignored and he could not even get an interview. He wondered whether he should give up as the constant rejections were making him lose confidence and he was aware of younger talent coming through even on his own station.

Andy carried out a basic Options Spread, but added the significance of the separate numbers and the overall number in the hope that this might offer a clue to his best option. His pack, the Universal Waite, had the Fool

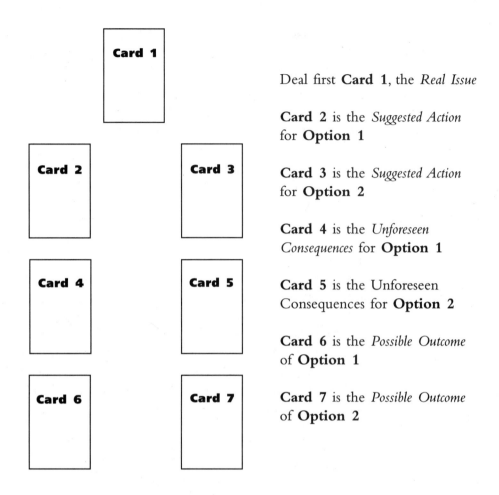

Deal first **Card 1**, the *Real Issue*

Card 2 is the *Suggested Action* for **Option 1**

Card 3 is the *Suggested Action* for **Option 2**

Card 4 is the *Unforeseen Consequences* for **Option 1**

Card 5 is the Unforeseen Consequences for **Option 2**

Card 6 is the *Possible Outcome* of **Option 1**

Card 7 is the *Possible Outcome* of **Option 2**

as 0. Remember to assign an option to each row before you deal the cards.

The first card you pick asks a specific question or identifies an area of concern: in Andy's case, what could he do about his career? Sometimes the options are not clear cut. As with the reading below, there can be two paths offering a different kind of fulfilment and it is important if you are reading for others not to influence the choice in any way, even if you are asked.

Card 1, *the question*, in the centre of the spread furthest away from you. **The Devil, 15**

Card 2 is the *suggested action* for **Option 1**: in Andy's case, should he push ahead to get to London? **The Tower, 16**

Card 3 is the *suggested action* for **Option 2**: should he remain where he is and develop other aspects of his life? **The Wheel of Fortune, 10**

Card 4 is the *unforeseen circumstances* for **Option 1. The Hanged Man, 12**

Card 5 is the *unforeseen consequences* for **Option 2. Death, 13**

Card 6 is the *possible outcome* of **Option 1. The Sun, 20**

Card 7 is the *possible outcome* of **Option 2. The Moon, 19**

Card 1, *the Question*: **The Devil, 15.** The number emphasises that in a sense he is imprisoning himself by false ideals and principles. London is the be-all and end-all for Andy and he feels that if he cannot make it there he is a failure, which may not be the case.

Option 1

Suggested action: **The Tower, 16**. So what is the prison from which Andy needs to escape? The number says where there has been seeming loss or stagnation, this can offer the basis for a much stronger relationship or situation, based on all the experiences gained through earlier pain or problems. So, rather than allowing his disappointment to slow him down, maybe Andy needs to go to London in a lesser capacity. Andy said he had been offered a job as a temporary researcher on one of the smaller radio stations, but felt this was a backward step as he was a senior presenter on his current station.

Unforeseen consequences of following the action in the previous card: **The Hanged Man, 12**. Number 12 implies that in spite of the loss of status, money and security, by pushing to the limits it is possible to break free of a repetitive cycle that may seem fruitless. In this case Andy was trapped in a double-bind: he could continue applying in vain for positions he cannot get or he could give up and stay in a job where he was increasingly frustrated. Once he was working in London, albeit at a less elevated level, he could acquire the skills and knowledge that would make his sacrifice worth while.

Possible outcome: **The Sun, 20.** The number of completion and through experience gained not only happiness and success in the near future, but also a new beginning as the cycle continues, so that in the future Andy would move even higher as he gained in confidence and know-how.

Option 2

Suggested action: **The Wheel of Fortune, 10.** In its number aspect the Wheel talks of natural cycles, destruction followed by creation and so this option is in a sense advising no action, but letting life take its course. This would suggest abandoning the London option for now or at least reducing the intensity of concentration and developing aspects within the current situation. Andy revealed that he had also been offered the opportunity to write, present and produce a series of features on local life and personalities which he had dismissed, but which would widen his perspectives and experience.

Unforeseen consequences of following the action in the previous card: **Death, 13.** This would seem an expected outcome and so the card must have deeper implications. Andy said he had sometimes wondered if the frantic world of modern music presenting was really for him and that he was aware that even if he did succeed in London, there was a whole part of himself that remained unexplored. Number 13, conventionally regarded as unlucky, could bring great fortune to Andy if it helped him to confront the deeper issue of what he wanted with his life, which was to work more with people; it could be that his documentaries might give him an opening into a different kind of work in which his knowledge rather than his personality could come to the fore.

Possible outcome: **The Hermit, 9**. A gateway to the unknown for Andy, not like the Fool's leap into the dark, but more measured, a deeper level, in Andy's case, of working perhaps in a more serious field. Because the Hermit is a symbol of withdrawal, it may suggest Andy will find the deep satisfaction that comes with this card number by entering a new cycle of his career and his personal development, based on the experience and knowledge he has acquired.

What should he do? Andy decided to discover the overall number of his reading before fully assessing the options.

He added together his seven card numbers:

$$15 + 16 + 12 + 20 + 10 + 13 + 9 = 95 = 9 + 5 = 14 = 5$$

The number 5, ruled by Mercury, is the number of versatility, communication and restlessness, endowing Andy with the ability to adapt to changing circumstances and to find alternative approaches if one fails, a love of adventure and travel, and the art of persuasion.

It is the number of the communicator, the messenger and born traveller. As the overall number in Andy's reading, it represents the desire to move on in some way, selling his own abilities if the move is to be advantageous.

Andy felt that this was telling him that deep down he knew he would never settle unless he at least tried London so he decided to take the job of temporary researcher and to find a way to presenting through that. As in this case numerology can offer a great deal of additional information, especially if a reading is not clear-cut.

MAKING A PERSONALISED READING

If a question is related to a particular date in your life, add together your date of birth and either the day of the reading or the future date, perhaps of an interview. This will give an immediate strategy.

Andy was born on 06/03/1963 and the date by which he had to accept or reject the temporary researcher's job offer was 12/02/1999.

$$6 + 3 + 63 + 12 + 2 + 99 = 185 = 14 = 5$$

This is the same as his overall strategy number, another confirmation that Andy is on track.

Chapter 11

The Tarot and Magic

Tarot cards are one of the most portable forms of magic and ritual. Because of its universal associations, the Tarot pack does provide authentic symbols both as a focus for attracting specific energies and as magical tools in formal and informal rites.

Magical ritual recognises the male/female energies in the forms of the Goddess and the Horned God which date back to the early Mother Goddess and her consort/son. The Horned God was the God, first of all, of the Hunt and Animals, and later the God of Vegetation and Corn who died annually with the harvest that he and the crops might be reborn (see my book *The Complete Guide to Magic and Ritual*, Piatkus, 1999).

The Emperor/Empress and the High Priestess/Hierophant are direct parallels to the male/female polarity in magic and can be used as a substitute for God and Goddess power statues. You may prefer to use the Empress and Emperor if your magic concerns relationships, love, family or money and the other two cards for more spiritual focuses. For specific people you can use the individual Court cards or cards that seem to relate most directly to the people concerned (see Chapter 2).

The Elements and the Tarot

The old alchemical elements of Earth, Air, Fire and Water that you have met in association with the Tarot suits are central to ritual and you can use the four Aces to represent the powers inherent in the elements. Each represents a direction and season. The attributes of the four elemental suits have already been mentioned in Chapter 3 on the Minor Arcana, so in this chapter I will add the magical properties.

ACE of PENTACLES

EARTH
Pentacles or Discs
The North, Winter and Midnight
Its colour is green or brown
The Pentacles symbolise the dish from which Jesus ate the paschal lamb. In Celtic tradition it represented the ancient Stone of Fal, on which the High Kings of Ireland stood to be crowned. The Stone was on Tara, the sacred Hill of the High Kings of Ireland· and before them the hero gods. In the seventh century the stone was taken to Scotland where it became the much-disputed Stone of Scone. For many years it was placed in the English coronation chair.

Earth is the element of order, both in nature and institutions such as the law, politics, finance, health and education. It represents the female, yin, nurturing goddess aspect, Mother Earth, the home and family as well as money and security. Its elemental creatures are gnomes, with their stores of hidden treasure, wisdom and above all common sense. You may see these fleetingly in your garden amid the autumn leaves.

Salt usually represents the substance of Earth as it is the purest element and vital for human life.

You can also use a dish of herbs or a flower or leaves from a tree, associated with the particular Major Arcana card that is the focus of the ritual.

The Ace of Pentacles will serve as your Earth tool and should be placed in the North in a 12 o'clock position on a clock face, in rituals.

AIR
Swords
The East, Spring and Dawn
Its colour is yellow

Swords symbolise the Sword of King David and, in Celtic tradition, the sword of Nuada of the Silver Hand whose sword hand was cut off in battle. With a new hand fashioned in silver he went on to lead his people to victory. Like the other Celtic elemental symbols it was one of the treasures of the Dagda, the Father God.

Air represents life itself, logic, the mind, communication, health, new beginnings, travel, learning and healing, and the male/yang/god in the form of sky deities. Its elemental creatures are sylphs, gentle spirits of the air, who can be seen fleetingly as butterflies and offer ideas, ideals and a reminder to enjoy happiness while you can.

Incense is the elemental substance of Air, with different perfumes used for different purpose in rituals, for example: allspice for money rituals; bay for rituals concerning health; cinnamon for increasing psychic awareness; Dragon's Blood for sexual attraction and fertility; frankincense for success and new beginnings; myrrh for endings and banishing sorrow; lavender or rose for love; pine for courage and cleansing; rosemary or sage for memory and learning; and sandalwood for protection. You can also use the incense associated with the Major Arcana card that is being used as a focus for the ritual. You will need a large fireproof container or an incense censer for moving it around the circle.

The Ace of Swords will serve as your initial tool for Air energies and should be placed at the 3 o'clock position on a clock face.

FIRE
Wands, Spears or Staves
The South, Summer and Noon
Its colour is red

Wands symbolise the sacred lance that pierced Jesus' side. In Celtic tradition it is the spear of Lugh, who slew his

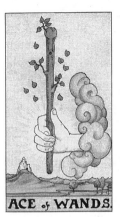

ACE of WANDS.

own grandfather, the old solar god Balor, with it and so brought about the new order.

Fire is Light, the Sun, lightning, fertility, power, joy, ambitions, inspiration and achievement and also destruction of what is now no longer needed. Like Air, it represents the male/yang/god in the form of the sun deities. The elemental creature is salamander, the mythical lizard (though the name is now given to a species of amphibious newt), which lives within fire.

Candles are the elemental substances of Fire, and are a potent symbol of different needs, according to the colour associated with the Tarot card used in a specific ritual (the colour associations are given later in this chapter). Use a broad-based candle holder so that you do not burn yourself when you move your candle during the ritual.

The Ace of Wands will serve as your ritual tool for Fire energies and should be placed in the 6 o'clock position on a clock face.

WATER

Cups or Chalices

The West, Autumn and Dusk

Its colour is blue

The Cups or Chalices are symbols of the Grail cup from which Jesus drank at the Last Supper, and the Cauldron of the Dagda, the Celtic father god, another of the great treasures, that was never empty and had great healing powers.

Water is the element of love, relationships, sympathy, intuition, healing, and the cycle of birth, death and rebirth. Like earth it represents the female/yin/goddess in the form of the Moon goddesses. Its elemental creatures are undines, spirits of the water. The original Undine was created without a soul, but gained one by marrying a mortal and bearing him a child. However, she also lost her freedom from pain and her immortality.

Water represents its own element. Use either pure spring water from a sacred spring or tap water left for a twenty-four hour cycle in a crystal or clear glass container

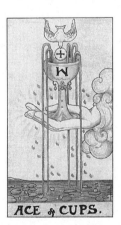

ACE of CUPS.

in the sun and moonlight. You can place it in a goblet or tall, narrow wine glass.

The Ace of Cups will serve as the tool of the Water element and should be placed in the 9 o'clock position on a clock face.

Tarot Spells

You can use your divinatory pack for Tarot magic and this will empower your cards. However, if you do want to carry out rituals over a period of days, it can be helpful to have a special pack which you reserve solely for magic and keep your divinatory pack for day-to-day use. Intrinsic to all magic is the concept of the magic circle, to mark out a space for carrying out rituals, concentrating power and providing a protective boundary against negative influences. Earth, Air, Fire and Water, representing law, life, light and love, are central to all ritual magic and in the Northern hemisphere are sited at the four compass points in any magic circle.

PSYCHIC PROTECTION

You can use any of the methods suggested for Tarot reading, especially the protection of sentinels of light or angels (as described in the Introduction to this book) to stand at the four compass points as you light each elemental candle.

Look into each flame and ask for the protection of the angel of that particular energy or Power of Light. If it helps, raise the card of Temperance if it portrays the Angel of the Rainbow above each candle and call the light into the card and by transference to yourself.

BEGINNING MAGIC

Before beginning any ritual or empowerment, spend a few minutes deciding on the precise purpose, not just for example, 'getting married' or 'prosperity', but 'to whom' and, for money, 'what for' and 'how much'. Magic works best when fuelled by need and emotion.

Needless to say all magic should have a positive purpose and should never be undertaken in anger. Neither should you attempt to call or bind others against their will, however apparently just the cause.

Magic comes back threefold so spells carried out in love and a spirit of giving will reap rewards in unexpected ways.

Major Arcana cards form the best focus for spells and later in the chapter I have listed purposes for which each card can be used, together with associated crystals, flowers, herb and oils so that you can empower any card in its unique way. Select a Major Arcana Tarot card that most closely corresponds with your need or wish.

CASTING THE CIRCLE

With Tarot spells, you can carry out the ritual on a table and either visualise a golden circle of light beginning in the North and continuing in an unbroken shape or draw a circle clockwise on paper beginning in the North.

- Find either magnetic North or symbolic North which should be in the direction you would face if you were looking towards a town north of your home.
- Place your four Aces in position beginning with the Ace of Pentacles in the North and then light four small candles, one to stand behind each card, in the appropriate elemental colour as listed above.
- You can create a larger circle clockwise, sun or clockwise in the earth or in sand with a rod cut from a hazel or rowan tree for wisdom and protection; alternatively draw a chalk circle in your yard or on a tiled floor. This can be large enough for one or more people and again place your cards at the four main compass positions.
- In a large circle, rest the cards on plates or dishes, a pewter or iron colour in the North, an aluminium one in the East, a brass or gold-coloured one in the South and silver

or copper in the West. Alternatively you can use circles of foil.

- Light taller candles if you are using a big circle. You may wish to place a small table in the centre on which to arrange your focal card plus the four elemental substances arranged in a square round it. If you are working with a small circle, leave the elemental substances at the compass points.

- Some traditions begin in the East, the direction of the rising sun, but many traditional forms of magic use the North as the source of power and face North as I have suggested here.

- When you have created your circle, place your elemental Aces in position and light the candles, set the chosen card in the centre of the circle, and create a picture in your mind's eye of the successful culmination of the aim of the ritual.

- Sprinkle a circle of salt around your card, seeing your wish having firm foundations and step by step moving closer to fruition. Invoke the power of the Earth in such words as: 'Mighty stone circles that have survived the test of time, great rocks that resist the battering of the seas, craggy mountains that stand firm though nations fall and gentle Mother Earth with your golden mantle, aid my endeavour.'

- Return the salt to its place and light next the incense fragrance associated with your card or Air, or an all-purpose incense such as frankincense or sandalwood. Pass the smoke clockwise around your card nine times, with such words as: 'Rushing winds who bring change and new life in your wake, swift eagle soaring upwards to the sun, aid my endeavour.'

- Return the incense to its position and leave it burning. Take the candle in the appropriate colour for your card or an all-purpose white candle and pass the card nine times clockwise around the candle flame, with such words as: 'Noonday Sun with your brilliant light and fertilising heat, searing lightning flashing through the midsummer sky making night as light as day, aid my endeavour.'

- Return the candle to its place and leave it to burn.
- Finally take the dish or cup of water and sprinkle water around your card. If you are using an oil burner, light it in advance and circle the card nine times around the steam, with such words as: 'Tumultuous oceans, wild rushing rivers, cascading waterfalls and life-giving rain, aid my endeavour.'
- Return the water to its position and take up the Ace of Pentacles. Place this across the focal card from North to South, slightly above so that it partially covers it, invoking the power of Pentacles, magical tool of the Earth element: 'Sacred Grail dish, stone of the High Kings of Ireland, let the strength, perseverance and sure foundations of the earth give structure to my desire.'
- Leaving the Ace of Pentacles in position, take the Ace of Swords and place this horizontally from East to West across the focal card, partially covering it and the Ace of Pentacles. Invoke the power of the Swords, magical tool of the Air element, with the words: 'Sword of David and the silver-handed warrior, bring logic, determination and clear communication to cut through inertia and obstacles in my path.'
- Leave the Ace of Swords in position and next take the Ace of Wands, putting this from South to North so that it overlaps the other cards. Invoke the power of Wands, the magical tool of the Fire element: 'Sacred spear of the Grail, weapon of the Light-bringer, endow certainty, inspiration and clarity to clear away the lingering dark shadows of doubt and despair.'
- Leave the Ace of Wands in position and finally set the Ace of Cups from West to East across the other cards. Invoke the power of the Cups, magical tool of the Water element: 'Healing waters of the Grail cup, cauldron of eternal nourishment, impart your intuitive wisdom to reconcile any differences of opinion and guide my course to a swift and harmonious conclusion.' You now need to concentrate the power of the ritual so that you can bring it to a climax and release the power into the cosmos, where it will attract

the energies you need to make your wishes come true. The two easiest ways are chanting and knot tying.

- You could focus on the accumulated power of the card pile reciting nine times, getting faster with each repetition: 'Earth, Air, Water, Fire, bring me now my heart's desire.'

- Such chants often seem trite on the page. The importance is to create a natural rhythm and some people drum along to or sing a chant to build up the intensity. The secret of powerful magic is in using the words of the heart.

- After the last chant snap your fingers or clap your hands over the cards, saying: 'The Power is Free, the wish is mine.'

- Alternatively, take a length of red wool and tie it in nine loose knots, in different places, reciting with increasing speed and intensity:

> *Knot one*
> *I bind my dream,*
> *Knot two*
> *I find new power,*
> *Knot three*
> *to wind this hour,*
> *Knot four*
> *The power is more,*
> *Knot five*
> *The spell's alive,*
> *Knot six*
> *My fate's not fixed,*
> *And as the knot is leaven*
> *I take control in Seven*
> *Knot eight*
> *My path is straight,*
> *Knot nine*
> *The wish is mine.*

- At this point you can either undo the knots in rapid succession, saying 'The power is free' or, if you have another Tarot pack for general use, leave the cards and knots in a safe place for nine days, undoing a knot each day to release the energies gradually, repeating the empowerment each time.

- When the ritual is done, before you remove your cards and knots, uncast the circle, anti-clockwise.
- Blow out your elemental candles in the reverse order of lighting, thanking your angels or sentinels for their protection.

At any time you need strength or encouragement in continuing the magical impetus in the everyday world, focus on your card and see in your mind's vision the elemental powers aiding your endeavour.

SECONDARY CARDS

You can use both Minor Arcana and Court cards to add significance to a ritual. You can select the appropriate Court cards for people in a love ritual, so that the Lovers card would stand in the centre with perhaps a Court card on either side.

From the Minor Arcana select cards that flesh out your need, for example the Eight of Wands for travel and perhaps the Six of Swords if the travel will take you away from a difficult situation. You can place as many or as few cards around your main focal card as you wish within the main circle and you make larger circles with your elemental substances and arrange your elemental cards so that they also partly cover the subsidiary cards.

Magical Associations

Each of the Major cards has animals, crystals (see also Chapter 7 on Crystals and the Tarot), flowers and trees, incense and herbs associated with them, and you can use these as a way of empowering a ritual or invoking the strength inherent in your card. These associations are taken from a variety of sources and are ones that I use regularly.

For flowers, trees and herbs use a similar species if the one listed is not indigenous to your region.

As well as using them in an actual spell, you can circle a card you choose whose strength you need at a particular time, with its associated crystals, flowers and other associations, for example a model or picture of the animal or even a feather.

Light the appropriate coloured candle and sit with the card and its attributes in the darkness. Then blow out the candle, sending the light to whoever needs it and sleep with your display next to your bed. This can be very helpful after you have used the card for meditation or astral work and may give you significant dreams.

THE FOOL

Candle colour: White
Creature: Salmon
Crystal: Clear crystal quartz
Flower: Primrose/crocus
Herb: Peppermint
Incense: Allspice
Oil: Sandalwood
Tree: Birch

For rituals for new beginnings, optimism, animals, babies and children and travelling light.

THE MAGICIAN

Candle colour: Yellow
Creature: Serpent
Crystal: Carnelian
Flower: Bracken/broom
Herb: Eyebright
Incense: Dragon's blood
Oil: Cinnamon
Tree: Ash

For all matters of the arts, business, communication, healing, psychic development and protection against trickery and theft.

THE HIGH PRIESTESS
Candle colour: Lilac
Creature: Owl
Crystal: Amethyst
Flower: Lily
Herb: Lavender
Incense: Bay
Oil: Cedarwood
Tree: Elder
For rituals concerning personal identity and spirituality, for secrets and for matters concerning younger people, especially women.

THE EMPRESS
Candle colour: Pink
Creature: She-wolf
Crystal: Jade
Flower: Myrtle
Herb: Yarrow
Incense: Geranium
Oil: Neroli
Tree: Peach or coconut
For rituals concerning domestic matters, fertility, motherhood, marriage, fidelity, family and middle-aged women.

THE EMPEROR
Candle colour: Deep blue
Creature: Eagle
Crystal: Turquoise
Flower: Chrysanthemum
Herb: Columbine or Solomon's seal
Incense: Frankincense
Oil: Marjoram
Tree: Oak
For rituals for power, courage, success, prosperity, career and middle-aged men.

THE HIEROPHANT
Candle colour: Purple
Creature: Spider
Crystal: Lapis lazuli
Flower: Orchid
Herb: Yarrow
Incense: Sage
Oil: Juniper
Tree: Walnut
For rituals concerning learning, knowledge, wisdom, finding lost objects, older people of both sexes and authority.

THE LOVERS
Candle colour: Green
Creature: Lovebirds
Crystal: Rose quartz
Flower: Forget me not
Herb: Vervain
Incense: Rose
Oil: Ylang-ylang
Tree: Cherry
For all relationships, especially love ones, for attracting loves, for choices in all matters and for sex.

THE CHARIOT
Candle colour: Scarlet
Creature: Swallow
Crystal: Rutilated quartz
Flower: Thistledown
Herb: Rosemary
Incense: Benzoin
Oil: Ginger
Tree: Sycamore
Rituals for travel, new ventures, house moves, resisting being pulled in different directions, self-confidence and independence.

STRENGTH
Candle colour: Burgundy
Creature: Ox
Crystal: Malachite
Flower: Cactus
Herb: Pennyroyal
Incense: Cedar
Oil: Basil
Tree: Blackthorn
Rituals for increasing physical and mental abilities and overcoming illness, patience and to overcome obstacles.

THE HERMIT
Candle colour: Grey
Creature: Turtle/crayfish
Crystal: Desert rose
Flower: Nasturtium
Herb: Blessed thistle
Incense: Thyme
Oil: Eucalyptus
Tree: Hawthorn
Rituals to prevent loneliness, for prophetic dreams, for starting again alone, for finding the way and for personal integrity.

THE WHEEL OF FORTUNE
Candle colour: Orange
Creature: Chameleon
Crystal: Cat's eye
Flower: Honeysuckle
Herb: Clover
Incense: Fern
Oil: Patchouli
Tree: Banyan
For rituals for prosperity and all money matters, good fortune and reversing a run of bad luck, for change of all kinds.

JUSTICE
Candle colour: Dark grey
Creature: Hawk
Crystal: Banded agate
Flower: Celandine
Herb: Cascara sagrada
Incense: Gum arabic
Oil: Lemon
Tree: Hazel
For rituals concerning negotiations, for decision-making, legal matters and any involving officialdom, releasing anger about earlier injustices.

THE HANGED MAN
Candle colour: Dark green
Creature: Pelican
Crystal: Bloodstone
Flower: Passion flower
Herb: Balm of Gilead
Incense: Clove
Oil: Tea tree
Tree: Aspen
For rituals concerning giving up compulsions and addictions, for beginning a new, difficult but ultimately rewarding path, for ending destructive relationships, for initiation into deeper understanding and psychic awareness, for accepting the inevitable as a learning experience.

DEATH
Candle colour: Dark brown or black
Creature: Phoenix
Crystal: Apache's tear (Obsidian)
Flower: White carnation
Herb: Rue
Incense: Myrrh
Oil: Camphor
Tree: Yew
For rituals concerning endings, life transitions, moves of

all kinds, leaving behind sorrow and regrets, laying old ghosts.

TEMPERANCE
Candle colour: Cream
Creature: Dove
Crystal: Blue lace agate
Flower: Iris
Herb: Angelica
Incense: Lilac
Oil: Chamomile
Tree: Olive

For harmony and personal happiness, for healing, moderating feelings, words or actions and for contacting your guardian angel or spirit guide.

THE DEVIL
Candle colour: Mustard yellow
Creature: Goat
Crystal: Red jasper
Flower: Marigold
Herb: Witch hazel
Incense: Copal
Oil: Pine
Tree: Cypress

For rituals for change, for releasing negative energies, integrating the shadow self into the personality, for psychic and physical protection against attacks and threats, for overcoming fears and free-floating anxiety.

THE TOWER
Candle colour: Dark yellow
Creature: Bat
Crystal: Leopardskin jasper
Flower: Peony
Herb: Sweet grass
Incense: Vanilla
Oil: Cedar

Tree: Holly

For removing restrictions and overcoming feelings of alienation, for sexual potency, material security, property matters, discovering secrets, protection at home, protection from natural hazards such as storms, and for new directions.

THE STAR

Candle colour: Pale yellow
Creature: Starfish
Crystal: Citrine
Flower: Mimosa
Herb: Star anise
Incense: Violet
Oil: Rosewood
Tree: Magnolia

For rituals concerning the granting of wishes and the fulfilment of dreams, for fame and stardom and all forms of recognition, the card of would-be writers, actors, entrepreneurs, musicians and dancers.

THE MOON

Candle colour: Silver
Creature: Hare
Crystal: Moonstone
Flower: Jasmine
Herb: Valerian
Incense: Mimosa
Oil: Lemongrass
Tree: Willow

For rituals concerning women and the cycles of life, for peaceful sleep, for beauty, for any attracting rituals on the waxing moon and banishing rituals on the waning moon, for spiritual development and access to other dimensions.

THE SUN

Candle colour: Gold
Creature: Lion

Crystal: Amber
Flower: Sunflower
Herb: St John's wort
Incense: Mandarin
Oil: Orange
Tree: Date palm

For rituals concerning happiness, success, energy, lofty ambitions, revealing hidden potential, travel to sunny places, renewal of health.

JUDGEMENT

Candle colour: Indigo
Creature: Falcon
Crystal: Falcon's eye
Flower: Orchid
Herb: Turmeric
Incense: Lemon verbena
Oil: Lime
Tree: Alder

For breaking free of guilt, for forgiveness and mending of quarrels, for finding the right career, all weighty official and financial matters, breaking free of critical people and self-esteem.

THE WORLD

Candle colour: Multi-coloured
Creature: Horse
Crystal: Aquamarine
Flower: Tiger lily
Herb: Parsley
Incense: Heather
Oil: Grapefruit
Tree: Apple

For rituals for the expansion of horizons, long-distance travel, promotion, freedom from the past, environmental and ecological issues, for self-confidence and a happy future.

Appendix 1

Turning Professional

There are no national or internationally recognised qualifications in Tarot reading. There are also many levels of being a professional reader, from doing occasional paid readings for people who have been recommended by friends or acquaintances to a full-blown business with a regular personal postal and telephone Tarot service and perhaps a spot on television or radio, plus several Tarot books to your name. There really are no limits, given perseverance, and if you find that people do comment on the accuracy of your Tarot readings almost from your first attempt, then you may have a natural gift for the Tarot that can lead to a new career as well as your personal spiritual evolution.

How to Begin

Once you are confident reading for friends and family, you can then begin to read for strangers. In many ways this is easier, as you do not try to fit the cards to your preconceptions of what they ought to be saying and you feel less inhibited. Trust the words you hear in your head and the sudden insights, even if they are not directly linked to the cards, for your intuitive wisdom that is speaking holds the key to any reading. The cards are the entry point, but as with your meditation, astral and past life work if you can walk through and beyond them in a reading, then you are no longer limited by logic and linear time.

There are many opportunities for Tarot readings that arise naturally, if you keep your Tarot pack with you; social occasions, at parties and at work or college. Casually mention your new interest to acquaintances or work colleagues, once you are sure they will not disapprove, as there is still some fear and suspicion associated with Tarot readings. But many people are fascinated and will ask you questions or to see the cards; usually they are surprised that the images are so beautiful and not spooky at all. Before long you will find you are inundated with requests for readings, although some people will wait until you are alone to ask. The sceptics are usually the most eager to have a reading.

Go to their homes or invite them to yours and make readings at this stage a social occasion.

Do not feel you have to prove anything. Explain that the cards are the focus for a psychic dialogue and that you will suggest meanings and the questioner can apply them. This is not an opt-out. No one would consult a doctor or dentist and expect him or her to guess what was wrong.

Before long you will find that relatives and friends of people for whom you have done readings will ask if you will read for them. But beware emotional leeches who demand magical answers, but are totally unwilling to help themselves.

Use the psychic protection described at the beginning of the book and cleanse your cards with a crystal or pendulum, especially after encountering negativity.

At this stage you will probably not want to charge for readings, but accept any gifts with thanks and if asked about a fee, mention you like flowers, essential oils or have a charity box in which people can put anonymous donations.

Testing your Expertise

Once you feel more confident and have confirmation that your readings are accurate, you will naturally relax and may become ready for a greater challenge. If not, do not feel pressurised. The majority of Tarot readers concentrate on friends, family and the lame ducks that seem to quack to their door and the problem is usually how to refuse politely if you arrive at a party to find a queue of would-be clients with their problems.

If you do want to test your skills further, volunteer to Tarot read for charity at a local fête. This will give you the experience of reading for a large number of people in rapid succession and tell you if you would enjoy working as a Tarot reader. I honed my skills reading the Tarot in bookshops while promoting books and on television and radio with calls every two or three minutes. I have found that when you get really tired you switch off and your intuition comes to the fore, sometimes giving quite remarkable results. However, this kind of work is exhausting in every way and if you do have a marathon session, afterwards you should switch off for at least twenty-four hours and allow your psychic energies to return naturally. Let your body be the guide. If you have a period of disturbed sleep or bad dreams and you feel as though every noise is drilling through your mind, it may be time to cut down on psychic work for a while and concentrate on physical activities.

This period of unpaid clairvoyance may last months. If sessions are more pleasurable than painful, you may be ready to turn professional. However, do not rush yourself. Charging for a reading can put great pressures on you to perform and for some people it destroys the joy and spirituality of the Tarot.

Turning Professional – The First Steps

The Tarot is such a personal, powerful activity that it is a very exhausting way of earning money if you do it properly and, like a counsellor, psychologist or priest, you'll come across many lifestyles you may not agree with. Unless you are incredibly experienced – and I don't think even a counselling course can prepare you for the intimacy of souls involved in good Tarot readings – you may find that even two in-depth readings are more than you can manage in a day, certainly initially.

However, if you do decide that you wish to use your gifts professionally, a bonus is that people suddenly start valuing your advice. A Siberian shaman commented that a client should always pay for healing, because otherwise it was not effective.

I have discovered myself that having given accurate free Tarot readings to strangers, acquaintances and friends alike, they will often say: 'That was brilliant. Now I will go to a proper Tarot reader as well [ie one who charges] to be sure.'

- Begin by charging a moderate amount to a stranger who comes to you via an acquaintance and asks what you charge.
- If this feels right, continue to obtain clients by word of mouth and when you are ready advertise in a New Age shop or a reputable New Age magazine, but use a PO Box for security.
- Be wary of admitting total strangers to your home if you are alone and, if you are a woman, get a man to record a message on your answerphone.
- Arrange appointment times in advance. People who are travelling to see you will probably want at least an hour – you may find that you need to explain your methods and any other Tarot tools you may use. Your Crystal Tarot is an excellent additional psychic tool or you could add the Kabbalah or even a regression using the Tarot method. The Tarot is in itself at the hub of a whole number of psychic skills and the multi-faceted approach is both powerful and fascinating to people who have only experienced conventional clairvoyance.
- You may wish to have a coffee percolator or kettle and a selection of herbal teas in the room where you are working as this can relax the client.
- Leave time either side so you can extend the session, if someone is talking over a problem, but establish early on a method of bringing a session to an end or you may end up talking in circles.
- Make sure you are not disturbed and create a calm atmosphere with candles or soft lights, oils and music so that you both feel relaxed.
- Many people who come for readings have a decision to make or are unhappy. Do not be tempted to promise new love or money to make them happier, but try to steer them to make small plans for step-by-step improvements. Try to limit readings with an individual to once a fortnight or week at the most as more frequent sessions can confuse matters and not give time for psychic and earthly efforts to bear fruit. You may need to wean some people off over-dependency as they become more reluctant to make any decisions without consulting you.
- Use an answerphone. I do talk to people when they ring if I can, but it is very disruptive for private life if you work from home.
- Some clients like tape recordings of the session, so get a good tape recorder and bulk buy cassettes. Use a two-way mike to place between you. If you are not used to hearing your own voice practise in advance so you will not feel inhibited or self-conscious.
- Give the name and date of the reading on tape in case the box gets lost and place a business card in each of the boxes. Charge the cost price of the tape.

- You are charging for your time and expertise and cannot nor should be expected to work miracles.

- If a client expresses dissatisfaction, try to help him or her to separate their disappointment with a Tarot message from your skills. If the client is still being difficult, charge half your normal fee and vow never to read for that person again. Some people are professional complainers. They will probably have visited at least a dozen other clairvoyants in the previous three months and expressed dissatisfaction with them all. They insist they have a perfect job, perfect relationship, wonderful children, plenty of money and total happiness, which raises the question of what they hope to gain from the reading. Usually the doubts will come tumbling out once you have overcome this defensiveness.

- At the end of your Tarot sessions, bathe in soothing oils such as lavender, mimosa or ylang-ylang and a psychically cleansing drop or two of pine or eucalyptus.

- Before you go to sleep, enclose yourself in a circle of pink light, using an amethyst or rose quartz to protect yourself from excess emotion and negativity and consciously push your clients' worries out of your mind so that you will enjoy a quiet sleep.

Financial Considerations

Psychic Fairs and Festivals of Healing offer excellent opportunities to try out your skills professionally in the wider field. See what other readers are charging and begin at the lower end of the scale. By the time you have paid for your stall, for business cards and travel, you may not have a great deal of profit to show for what is incredibly hard work, but you will have learned a great deal about your craft and hopefully helped a number of people. You can also use these events to build up a list of clients either for personal or postal readings and to make contacts with stall holders and other clairvoyants who can advise you which festivals are well organised and worth attending.

Once you are working professionally on a regular basis, you will need to pay self-employed National Insurance contributions which you can do through your local Social Security Office. You need also to declare your earnings for tax purposes to the Inland Revenue. This brings the advantage that you can set expenses against income, for example travel either to fairs or to clients' homes, the printing of any advertising material, stationery, telephone calls for business purposes and, if you work from home, a proportion of such expenses as heating and lighting.

Appendix 2

Tarot packs

The Standard Decks

These are most commonly used by clairvoyants and to illustrate Tarot books.

Rider Waite, the definitive and most popular deck, based on the Golden Dawn Tradition and beautifully illustrated by Pamela Coleman-Smith: a very detailed Minor Arcana. Also in mini and large format. One of the best learning packs.

Universal Waite, based on Pamela Coleman-Smith's illustrations, redrawn by Mary Hanson-Roberts, who has also created her own very pleasing Tarot pack. Almost identical images to the Rider Waite but softer and, some say, more artistic.

Aquarian Deck, of the Rider Waite genre, but more sophisticated and, to me, less vibrant. Good for beginners.

Marseilles, this classic Tarot deck is based on one used in France in the eighteenth century, with a wood-cut Major Arcana and Court cards and unadorned Minor Arcana.

Classic Deck, similar to the Marseilles, but with more pronounced and, some say, grotesque figures.

JJ Swiss Tarot, resembles the Tarot of Marseilles, has French titles on the cards.

Fantasy Tarots

Arthurian Tarot, in search of the Holy Grail, with symbolism rooted in the legends and traditions of Arthurian Britain, including Merlin, Guinevere and the Lady of the Lake. Good for those who love poetic images. The deck has a full-colour Celtic Cross layout sheet. It is excellent for magic.

Faery Wicca Tarot, contains the legends of Old Ireland and is rooted in the Faery Wiccan tradition with brilliant paint-box colours.

Lord of the Rings Tarot, a popular deck with Tolkien enthusiasts, but it does have book captions on the cards and has been said by critics to resemble a game rather than a Tarot set.

The Merlin Tarot, a good Tarot if you enjoy fantasy books with dragons and magicians, although the Major Arcana is far more beautiful than the Minor cards. The Major cards are excellent for meditation and past life work.

Morgan Greer, one of my favourites, has a fairy tale quality, excellent for past life work and rituals.

Russian Tarot of St Petersburg, the cards are based on a series of miniature paintings of Russian people and fairy tales.

Shakespearian Tarot, draws on characters from the plays with, for example, Romeo and Juliet. Quotations from the plays on each card add or detract, according to your viewpoint.

Tarot of the Cat People, for cat lovers. Even the Chariot is pulled by cats. Cats, leopards and lions are the companions of the colourful Cat People.

William Blake Tarot, inspired by the artwork of the painter/poet William Blake and uses collages of reproductions of his work. Good for meditation and astral travel work.

Historical Tarots

El Gran Tarot Esoterico, my own favourite, not strictly historical, but a Spanish Romany gypsy pack with a brilliantly coloured Major Arcana that captures the essence of the traditional gypsy world. The names are in Spanish but are relatively easy to follow, although the explanatory leaflet is in Spanish or French. The Minor Arcana is illustrated with simple symbols accompanying the very clear numbering.

Scapini Tarot, a very authentic and beautiful medieval design, with cards in the style of the classic Marseilles pack.

Tarot de Paris, an early seventeenth-century

deck, this is very beautiful and relatively easy to use, although the titles are in French.

Visconti-Sforza Tarrochi Deck, based on an original mid-fifteenth-century pack, this is a beautiful deck, but very large and so difficult to shuffle. The cards do not have names or numbers and can be confusing to interpret for beginners. However, it is a very powerful deck once a reader is more experienced.

Old English Tarot, a medieval English-style artwork with standard Tarot symbols.

Modern Tarots

Adrian Tarot, uses digitally edited photographic images with thin white line drawings overlaid on the images which are somewhat lacking in detail.

Arcus Arcanum, brightly coloured comic-book artwork but stays close to traditional suits. Popular with men.

The Renaissance Tarot, the Jane Lyle version, based on alchemical and Renaissance symbols in a new visionary form.

Rohrig Tarot, a glossy, up-to-the-moment deck, with, for example, the Chariot depicted as a Formula One racing car.

Stick Figure Tarot, a minimalistic Tarot *par excellence*, with basic Tarot symbols, treated with a sense of fun.

Mythological Tarots

Ancestral Path Tarot, draws on traditional Native American, feudal Japanese, Arthurian English and Egyptian symbols and images. A good starter pack in spite of the multi-cultural aspect.

Celtic Tarot, features figures from the Celtic tradition, the deities and the myths, with lovely Celtic knot work, rich colours and intricate detail.

Chinese Tarot, traditional Oriental artwork, but because it follows traditional Tarot symbolism suits can be used even by beginners.

Motherpeace, large round cards, not for those new to the Tarot, the suits draw from Native Spiritual traditions and are miniature works of art. They do correspond in many ways to traditional Tarot concepts. Cannot be shuffled, but for a second set for an experienced reader, the Motherpeace deck is one of my favourites. Excellent for meditation and astral projection.

Mythic Astrology Deck, a beautifully illustrated deck and book set, a good introduction to astrology using the sun, moon, planets and ascendants, but is not a set for learning the basic Tarot.

Mythic Tarot Deck, a good standard deck for learning, with a detailed Minor Arcana. It uses illustrations from Ancient Greek mythology of gods and goddesses, heroes and villains.

Norse Tarot, Viking myths with deities, warriors and runic images. It seems at odds with the Tarot concept, but is quite workable.

Symbolic Tarots

Alchemical Tarot, a relatively modern deck based on the spiritual alchemy of the Rosicrucians, with rich alchemical symbolism.

Golden Dawn Tarot, based on the Order of the Golden Dawn and therefore excellent for magic, meditation or the Kabbalah.

Hermetic Tarot, a black-and-white detailed set, recreating the esoteric Tarot deck of Mathers, one of the original members of the Golden Dawn.

Medicine Woman, a Native American based pack, drawing on the beauty and harmony of Mother Earth with artwork in pastel shades.

Native American Tarot, a mixture of authentic Native American traditions drawn from different tribes and the creator's own vision.

Navigators of the Mystic Sea, based on the Golden Dawn's interpretation of Kabbalah and so good for making links between the two systems. This deck is quite difficult to obtain and has very original, vivid artwork.

Sacred Rose Tarot, a colourful Tarot with Kabbalistic symbolism, merged with a standard deck.

Sante Fe Tarot, the best deck for pure Native American symbolism, drawing especially on the Navajo tradition.

Tarot of the Goddess, develops the Maiden, Mother and Crone concept, using images from Middle Eastern, Indian and Sumerian mythology.

Thoth Tarot, a Crowley deck with strong, some say frightening, and explicit artwork, good for Kabbalah work, but though a classic deck, better for those who have used the Tarot for some years.

Witches Tarot, a Pagan/Wiccan emphasis and strong links with the Kabbalah.

Aces 78
Adam 24, 28
air 7
alchemy 32
amber 159
amethyst 150
Amon 33
anima 21, 68, 69
animus 21, 68, 69
Anubis 33
Apache's tear 156
Apollo 29
aquamarine 159
Arcana 21
Archangels 9
    Gabriel 9
    Michael 9
    Raphael 9
    Uriel 9
archetypes
    connecting with 167
Aries 27
Artemis 41
astral projection 168
Astrological Wheel of Fortune 143
astrology 1
Babel 39
banded agate 155
Bibliotheque National in Paris 3
bloodstone 155
blue lace agate 156
Brigid 24
Buddhist philosophy 32
Cabalah 177
card of the day
    choosing 12
carnelian 150
cat's eye 154
Ceres 25
Cerridwen 25
Chariot 29
    astrological associations 134
    crystal associations 152
    gateway card 171
    Kabbalistic associations 197
    magical associations 235
    numerological associations 209
Charles V of France 3
choosing a spread 100
citrine 158

clairvoyance 5
cleansing your pack 7
Coleman-Smith, Pamela 4
collective unconscious 6, 27, 32,
    173
confronting life, cards of
    Chariot 28
    Lovers 28
    Strength 28
confronting mortality, cards of 34
    Death 35
    Hanged Man 34
    Temperance 36
Corn God 211
Constant, Alphonse Louis 4
Court cards 47
    defining 49
    fitting them into your world 73
    identifying the 50
Court de Grebelin, Antoine 3
creative cards 21, 41, 43
    Chariot 29
    Devil 37
    Emperor 26
    Fool, the 22
    Hierophant 27
    Justice 34
    Lovers 28
    Magician 23
    Star 39
crystal Tarot 147
    reading your 160
crystals, 8, 146
Cups
    Ace 79
    Eight 94
    Five 88
    Four 86
    King 64
    Knight 56
    Nine 96
    Page 51
    Queen 60
    Seven 92
    Six 90, 103
    Ten 98
    Three 84
    Two 82
Death 5, 35, 220
    astrological associations 135

crystal associations 56
    Kabbalistic associations 200
    numerological associations 211
    magical associations 237
Demeter 25
desert rose 152
Devil 5, 28, 37, 70, 104
    astrological associations 136
    crystal associations 157
    Kabbalistic associations 201
    numerological associations 212,
        218
    magical associations 238
Divine Child 42
dreaming and doing, cards of
    Moon 40
    Sun 41
Earth 7
Eights 93
elements (Earth, Air, Fire and Water)
    48, 223–226
Eliot, T.S. 22
Emperor 26
    astrological associations 133
    crystal associations 151
    Kabbalistic associations 196
    numerological associations 208
    magical associations 234
empowering your pack 8
Empress 22, 25
    astrological associations 139
    crystal associations 151
    gateway card 170
    Kabbalistic associations 195
    magical associations 234
    numerological associations 208
Eve 24, 28
external power, cards of
    Emperor 26
    Empress 25
    Hierophant 27
falcon's eye 159
Fire 7
Fives 87
Fool 22, 26, 27, 30, 31, 32, 34, 214
    astrological associations 141
    gateway card 170
    crystal associations 149
    Kabbalistic associations 194
    numerological associations 207

magical associations 233
Force 31
Fortitude 31
Fortuna 33
fortune telling 119
Fours 85
Freud, Sigmund 38
Frigg 25
gateway cards 170
Golden Dawn, Order of 4, 127
Graves, Robert 4
Grim Reaper 36
Hanged Man 26, 34, 129
  astrological associations 142
  crystal associations 155
  kabbalistic associations 199
  magical associations 237
  numerological associations 211
hawk's eye 159
Helios 41
Henry V 48
Hermes 23
Hermes Trismegistus 32
Hermit 28, 31, 33, 221
  astrological associations 135
  crystal associations 152
  gateway card 171
  Kabbalistic associations 198
  magical associations 236
  numerological associations 210
Hierophant
  astrological associations 133
  crystal associations 152
  gateway card 170
  Kabbalistic associations 196
  magical associations 235
  numerological associations 208
High Priestess 24
  astrological associations 150
  crystal associations 150
  gateway card 170
  Kabbalistic associations 195
  magical associations 234
  numerological associations 208
Higher Self 28
history of Tarot 2
Holy Grail 5
Knights 30
Id 38
Inner Child 69, 71
inner powers, cards of your
  Fool 22
  High Priestess 24
  Magician 23
jade 151
Jesus 25
Joseph 26
journal 13
Judgement 42
  astrological associations 143
  crystal associations 159
  Kabbalistic associations 203

magical associations 240
  numerological associations 213
Jung, Carl Gustav 6, 47
  archetypes, theory of 67
Justice 34
  Astrological associations 135
  crystal associations 155
  Kabbalistic associations 199
  magical associations 237
  numerological associations 210
Kabbalah 1, 4, 177
  divination 182
  lighting up the Tree of Life 205
  Major Arcana 179
  Minor Arcana 180
  pathways 180
  Sephiroth 184
  Tarot pathways 193
King Sol 22, 28, 40, 43
Kings 62
  Cups 64
  Pentacles 63
  Swords 66
  Wands 65
Knights 54
  Cups 56
  Pentacles 55
  Swords 58
  Wands 57
lapis lazuli 152
leopardskin jasper 158
Levi, Eliphas 4, 179
light and darkness, cards of
  Devil 37
  Star 39
  Tower 38, 37
  light, breathing in 166
Loki 37
Lovers, 28, 38, 105
  astrological associations 133
  crystal associations 152
  Kabbalistic associations 196
  magical associations 235
  numerological associations 209
Ma'at 34
Magi 40
magic 223
  casting the circle 228
  Tarot spells 227
Magician 23
  astrological associations 139
  crystal associations 150
  gateway card 170
  Kabbalistic associations 194
  magical associations 233
  numerological associations 194
Major Arcana 6, 12, 21
Malachite 153
Mars 27, 29
Marseilles Tarot 3
meditation 163
mediumship 5

Mercury 23
Minor Arcana 12, 74
  interpreting the numbers 78
Moon 40, 42
  astrological associations 137, 139
  crystal associations 159
  gateway card 171
  Kabbalistic associations 202
  magical associations 239
  numerological associations 213
Moon Goddess 40
moonstone 159
Mother Goddess 10, 24, 25
new horizons, cards of
  Judgement 42
  World 43
Nines 95
Norns 122
numerology 1, 206
  Andy's reading 217
  Major Arcana 207
  numbers in Tarot readings 214
  personalised reading 221
Odin 35
origins of Tarot 2
Pages 50
  Cups 51
  Pentacles 51
  Swords 53
  Wands 52
Pan 38
past life exploration 173
  mirror and candle technique 174
pendulum 13
Pentacles 224
  Ace 79
  Eight 93, 104
  Five 87
  Four 85
  King 63
  Knight 55
  Nine 95
  Page 51
  Queen 59
  Seven 92
  Six 89
  Three 83
  Two 81, 104
Piedmontese Tarot 3
planning ahead 123
Pope Joan 24
psychic development 163
psychic protection 8, 227
Pythagoras 206
Pythagoreans 206
Qabalah 177
Queen Luna 22, 28, 40, 43
Queens 58
  Cups 60
  Pentacles 59
  Swords 62
  Wands 61

Quetzelcoatl 42
Re 41
reacting to fate, cards of 31
  Hermit 31
  Justice 34
  Wheel of Fortune 32
reading for others 10
reading for yourself 11
reading Tarot suits 75
receptive cards 21
  Empress 25
  Hanged Man 34
  High Priestess 24
  Judgement 42
  Moon 40
  Strength 30
  Tower 38
  Wheel of Fortune 32
red jasper 157
reversed cards 13
Rider Waite 22
rose quartz 152
rutilated quartz 152
salamander 53
sandalwood 12
Seater 27
Sevens 91
shadow side 68, 69
significators 13
Sirius 40
Sixes 89
snakeskin jasper 158
special events 124
spreads
  astrological 131
  Astrological Wheel of Fortune
    145
  calendar 125
  Celtic Cross 112
  Court Card reading 108
  Earth, Air, Fire and Water 108
  Gestalt 101
  Karen's reading 102
  gypsy love card 71
  horseshoe 105
  Jungian 67
  mystical seven 107
  pyramid 110
  six weeks ahead 124
  Trisha's reading 69
  Web of Norns 122
St Michael 43
Star 39
  astrological associations 137
  crystal associations 158
  gateway card 171
  Kabbalistic associations 202

numerological associations 213
  magical associations 239
Strength 30
  astrological associations 134
  crystal associations 152
  Kabbalistic associations 197
  magical associations 236
  numerological associations 209
suits and relationships 72
Sun 41, 213, 220, 239
  astrological associations 138
  crystal associations 159
  gateway card 171
  Kabbalistic associations 203
  magical associations 239
  numerological associations 203
Sun signs 131
Swords 224
  Ace 80
  Eight 95
  Five 89
  Four 87
  King 66
  Knight 58
  Nine 97
  Page 53, 104
  Queen 62, 69
  Seven 93
  Six 91
  Ten 99
  Three 85
  Two 83, 104
synchronicity 6
Tara 4
Tariqua 4
Taro, River 3
Tarot journal 13
Tarrochi 3
Tauret 4
telepathy 6
Temperance 36
  astrological associations 136
  crystal associations 156
  gateway card 171
  Kabbalistic associations 200
  magical associations 238
  numerological associations 212
Tens 97
Thoeris 4
Thoth 3
Threes 83
time 123
Torah 4, 24
Tower 38, 105
  astrological associations 140
  crystal associations 158
  Kabbalistic associations 201

magical associations 238
  numerological associations 212
tribal voice 6
turning professional 241
  testing your expertise 242
turquoise 151
Twos 81
Universal Waite 22
Venetian Tarot 3
Venus 28
Virgin Mary 25
Waite Tarot 4
Waite, Arthur Edward 4
Wands
  Ace 80, 104
  Eight 94
  Five 88
  Four 86
  King 65
  Knight 57, 69
  Nine 96
  Page 52
  Queen 61, 69
  Seven 92
  Six 90
  Ten 98
  Three 84
  Two 82
Water 7
Web of the Tarot 121
Wheel of Birth, Death and Rebirth
  32
Wheel of Fortunes 32
  astrological associations 140
  crystal associations 154
  gateway card 171
  Kabbalistic associations 198
  magical associations 236
  numerological associations 210,
  219, 220
Wheel of the Year 33
Wordsworth, William 22
World 43
  astrological associations 141
  crystal associations 159
  gateway card 171
  Kabbalistic associations 204
  magical associations 240
  numerological associations 214
World Tree 35
Yeats, W.B. 4
your personal Tarot story 44
Zeus 27
zodiac 127
  planets and Tarot cards 137
zodiac wheel 128

BOOKS BY THE CROSSING PRESS

Pocket Guide To Astrology

By Alan Oken

Astrology serves as a way to explain events in life that otherwise appear inexplicable or arbitrary. This Pocket Guide covers the twelve signs of the zodiac and what they mean, the planets and how they affect your life, and the Houses and their role in your experience.

$6.95 • Paper • ISBN 0-89594-820-6

Pocket Guide to Fortunetelling

By Scott Cunningham

Pocket Guide to Fortunetelling is a complete guide to determining your past, present, and future. With detailed instructions of over 100 techniques, we find that this ageless art is a powerful ally in reshaping our lives.

$6.95 • Paper • ISBN 0-89594-875-3

Pocket Guide to Numerology

By Alan Oken

Discover the science of numerology. Each chapter begins with a simple formula that helps you discover your personal destiny, understand aspects of your character, or determine the proper time to accomplish a goal

$6.95 • Paper • ISBN 0-89594-826-5

Pocket Guide to The Tarot

By Alan Oken

The Tarot has been an ancient source of wisdom and insight into the human heart and mind. The 78 cards of the Tarot deck help you to open a door to higher consciousness, gain insights on the past and present, and discern future directions.

$6.95 • Paper • ISBN 0-89594-822-2

Pocket Guide to Wicca

By Paul Tuitean & Estelle Daniels

Wicca is a modern version of an ancient pagan sacred tradition that predated Christianity. It is Earth-, Nature-, and Fertility-oriented. This guide provides a comprehensive introduction to anyone interested in the Craft.

$6.95 • Paper • ISBN 0-89594-904-0

Pocket Guide to Shamanism

By Tom Cowan

Are you intrigued by the mysteries of nature and the realm of the spirit? Have you experienced a magical or mystical occurrence? Perhaps shamanism is calling you. Bringing shamanism into your life can allow you to restore sacred ritual, gain insight, and live with sensitivity and respect for the planet.

$6.95 • Paper • ISBN 0-89594-845-1

To receive a current catalog from The Crossing Press
please call toll-free, 800-777-1048.
Visit our Web site: **www.crossingpress.com**